Paul Gayler is one of the
the new generation. Trai
disciplines, he began coc...
late 1970s and was soon talent-spotted by Anton
Mosimann, who offered him the position of sous-
chef at the Dorchester. He subsequently became
head chef at the innovative and highly regarded
Inigo Jones, extending his repertoire by working in
Chinese and Indian restaurants. He is now executive
chef at the Lanesborough on Hyde Park, yet
describes himself as 'an eternal apprentice,
constantly learning, always developing my art.'

Paul has featured in BBC-TV's *Hot Chefs* and is a
regular guest presenter on *This Morning*. His first
book, *Virtually Vegetarian*, was published in 1995.
He lives in Leigh-on Sea with his wife and children.

GREAT VALUE GOURMET

meals and menus for £1

Paul Gayler

ORION

AN ORION PAPERBACK

First published in Great Britain by
Weidenfeld & Nicolson in 1996
This revised and expanded paperback edition
published in 1997 by Orion Books Ltd, Orion House,
5 Upper St Martin's Lane, London WC2H 9EA

Printed and bound in Great Britain by
The Guernsey Press Co. Ltd, Guernsey, C.I.

CONTENTS

Introduction   1

The Storecupboard   4

Thoughtful Shopping with the Seasons   9

A Few Remarks about Menu Planning   14

Soups   17

Starters and Salads   33

Pasta & Co   61

Main Courses   77

Vegetarian Dishes   107

Puddings   123

Index   151

INTRODUCTION

The idea behind this book stemmed from a telephone call I received at the Lanesborough one Friday morning in September 1995. Simon Hinde, the Consumer Affairs Correspondent of the *Sunday Times* rang me to ask if I was prepared to take up the challenge of devising a three-course menu for a family of four, with a budget of just £1. The idea behind this article, he told me, was to bring to people's attention the growing number of discount stores popping up all over Britain, such as Aldi and Lidl, who are offering food prices that are considerably undercutting the well-known supermarket chains.

At first I thought the idea absurd; what could possibly be prepared for £1? However, since my resolve and professionalism had been challenged, I felt that I could not refuse. I set about finding out more. Simon faxed me a list of some 10–12 discounted items he had purchased himself, such as canned beans, canned plum tomatoes, bread, milk, sausages. Even so, the saving grace was that I was allowed a basic storecupboard of ingredients that one might find in any home.

My menu, after much thought and toying with prices on my calculator, consisted of a spicy Mexican-style soup made from baked beans, followed by fusilli with hot dog sausages, tomatoes and herbs and, to finish, a cinnamon-infused baked apple. The whole menu was simplicity itself, well flavoured and reasonably priced, in fact only 87 pence for three courses. A little chilli for the soup, a few dried herbs for the pasta and cinnamon for the apples had worked wonders. I felt quite pleased with myself, but Simon wanted to put the menu to a further test.

He arranged for a family of four to dine at the Lanesborough to eat my 87p meal. The two adults and their two children arrived early one evening at the hotel, a little sceptical of what could be achieved with 100 pence.

After meeting them I returned to the kitchen determined to impress my guests. I'm glad to say the meal proved to be a great success – in fact they even asked for the soup recipe. The children left their plates clean, and having four children of my own, I know that this can sometimes be an achievement in itself.

The publicity that the article in the following weekend's *Sunday Times* attracted was hard to conceive. It made headlines in both American and Mexican newspapers and I received telephone calls from fellow chefs, readers, and even an Italian TV network.

Three months later I began to create this book on similar lines to my challenge; with the aid of a basic storecupboard, I set out to produce menus that vary from £1 for four to £1 per person. The recipes follow my passion for food from around the world, taking their inspiration from Mexico through Europe to the Far East.

Nowadays, thanks to price wars in all the major food outlets, simple but interesting meals are within the grasp of any home cook on a budget. Making the most of seasonal ingredients, the best quality convenience foods and a little imagination, cheap need never mean boring. Used creatively, herbs, spices and condiments add flavour to cheaper cuts of fresh meat and shellfish. Most of the recipes in this book are fairly easy to prepare and incredibly easy on the pocket.

All the recipes are for 4 people unless stated otherwise. I hope that you enjoy trying them.

Paul

THE **STORECUPBOARD**

Home cooking has changed dramatically over the past decade. A steady stream of television programmes celebrating food and foreign travel, backed up by magazine articles and advertisements, has opened our eyes to the many flavours the world has to offer. We also love to eat out and experience new foods at every opportunity. This new-found interest is reflected in our storecupboards; they are now likely to contain many more unusual ingredients – sauces, spices, herbs, different types of rice and pasta – than they would have done a few years ago.

So, what constitutes a basic storecupboard? In a way, it is impossible to summarize, since so much depends on the style of food that you personally enjoy and generally cook at home. However, one thing is for certain: a well-stocked cupboard will open the door to a greater choice of imaginative and exotic meals that the home cook can prepare easily and without further expense.

The following lists constitute what I personally consider a staple storecupboard (in fact, this is more or less what is in my cupboard at home). All the items are featured in the recipes within this book, some far more frequently than others. There's no need to rush out and spend a fortune on stocking up: you will already have many of the ingredients, and others can be bought when you need them.

Everyday basics
These are found in most households:
> salt, black pepper (preferably in a pepper mill, ready to be freshly ground, giving a far superior flavour to ready-ground pepper), vegetable oil (buy a neutral-flavoured oil such as sunflower oil for frying and general use), olive oil (choose extra virgin olive oil for use in dressings and sauces), butter (margarine has its uses, but cannot compare with the flavour of butter), milk (semi-skimmed is healthier than full-fat), eggs, plain flour, white and brown sugar, bread, tea, coffee.

Sauces and condiments
These are my favourite flavour enhancers:
> good-quality mayonnaise, light soy sauce, tomato ketchup, tomato purée, pesto sauce, Worcestershire sauce, Tabasco sauce, anchovy essence, capers in brine, black olives, white and red wine vinegar, balsamic vinegar, curry paste, mustard, horseradish, tahini paste.

Chicken, vegetable and beef stock are invaluable in the kitchen. Some supermarkets now sell good-quality ready-prepared stocks, but don't be afraid to use a stock cube – it's fine for many purposes.

Perishables
The vegetable rack and fruit bowl could include:
> fresh garlic, onions, spring onions, carrots, celery, leeks, potatoes, fresh ginger, lemons, oranges.

In the refrigerator you might also keep orange juice, a well-wrapped piece of Parmesan cheese, natural yoghurt and vegetarian suet.

Perishable in the sense that it gets eaten as soon as bought, unless well hidden, chocolate is also useful as an ingredient. Buy good-quality plain chocolate.

Herb and spice rack

Dried herbs are no substitute for fresh. If at all possible, I recommend that you start your own herb garden, which might include parsley, chives, mint, thyme and sage. The following dried herbs are acceptable if fresh herbs are not available:

bay leaf, thyme, sage, oregano, rosemary, mixed herbs.

Spices from around the world give dishes hot or subtle flavours and great depth of taste. Most spices tend to lose their flavour quite quickly once they have been ground; it is best to buy whole spices (seeds or pods) and grind them yourself just before using them. Alternatively, buy ground spices in small quantities – this is one occasion when it is a false economy to buy in bulk. I use a lot of spices, and the following are some of my favourites:

dried chilli flakes, cayenne pepper, paprika, coriander seeds, cumin, cinnamon, cardamom, nutmeg, cloves, caraway seeds, allspice, turmeric, ground ginger.

Ready-prepared spice mixtures, such as mild curry powder and garam masala, are also useful.

Fennel seeds, sesame seeds and Chinese five-spice powder appear once or twice in this book, and are worth buying if you are particularly fond of Indian or Chinese cooking.

Not just for cakes

Dried fruit and nuts can also be used in savoury dishes, and to add a touch of luxury to simple puddings:

cornflour, baking powder, vanilla essence, yeast (I prefer to use fresh yeast, although dried yeast is easier to keep as a standby – however, don't

keep it too long or it may lose its efficacy),
raisins, sultanas, prunes, walnut halves, whole
and flaked almonds, desiccated coconut.

Cans
These items can be lifesavers, and can easily be
converted into new and exciting dishes:
plum tomatoes (whole and chopped, in various
sizes), baked beans, sweetcorn, black beans,
cannellini beans, chickpeas, coconut milk, tuna,
herrings, sardines, red salmon, anchovy fillets.

Jars
The sweet-toothed may have these already, but several
of them can also be used to create savoury dishes:
good-quality raspberry and apricot jam, redcurrant
jelly, orange marmalade, clear honey, maple syrup,
peanut butter, molasses.

Pasta and grains
Dried pasta is always a good storecupboard standby
and other grains also make satisfying meals:
long rounded pasta such as spaghetti or linguine;
flat noodles such as trenette or tagliatelle; lasagne;
small pasta shapes such as fusilli, penne, rigatoni,
macaroni; a selection of different types of rice
might include long-grain white rice and brown
rice (for salads and general purposes), basmati
(a particularly fragrant rice with long thin grains),
arborio (a rounded grain rice, used to make
risotto); other grains that are good for absorbing
sauces include polenta (cornmeal) and couscous.

Drinks cabinet
I have long been of the opinion that a dish without
booze – in it, with it, or both – is somehow incom-
plete! One glass for the pot and one for the chef is

one of my favourite rules of the kitchen. Joking
aside, wines and spirits are invaluable in cooking,
especially the following:

> dry white wine, red wine, port, brandy, rum,
> sherry (a splash of dry sherry is often used in
> Chinese stir-fries), madeira, beer.

The freezer

I have never been a great advocate of the freezer – it's
a point of professional pride – but I do use it to store
food that has a very short season when fresh, such as
sweetcorn, peas and broad beans. I also find it convenient for storing some pasta, and puff and filo pastry.

It is well worth keeping a stock of ice cream –
vanilla and chocolate – to prepare simple desserts and
to serve as an accompaniment to hot or cold puddings.

THOUGHTFUL SHOPPING
WITH THE **SEASONS**

In a professional kitchen, chefs have access to good-quality raw materials on a daily basis from a varying list of suppliers. This means we can offer our clientele all their favourite foods throughout the year. To many people this may sound wonderful, but I find it somewhat sad, because I believe in the idea of seasonality in foods.

Nowadays, the larger supermarkets are also crammed full of exotic foodstuffs flown in from around the globe, thanks to advances in transportation and the higher expectations of shoppers.

Tomatoes, asparagus and strawberries, for example, are now available throughout the year. Tomatoes have often been picked far too early, therefore they lack flavour because they are under-ripe. The ripening process continues on their transportation to our markets, instead of on the vine where they should remain until ripe. Taste the difference between these tomatoes and those picked in the height of the summer season. They not only taste better, but they are also less expensive because they are plentiful. The same can be said of strawberries, asparagus and many other ingredients.

A market or greengrocer is far more likely than a supermarket to reflect the seasons – with lower prices when there is a glut. In a nutshell, if you cook with the seasons in mind, you will eat better and spend less. Shop often and plan your menus accordingly.

SPRING

For me the best spring dishes are simple, reflecting the delicacy of the new season, but are nonetheless full of fresh tastes and bright colours.

The glowing reds and distinctive flavours of rhubarb (outdoor-grown by late spring) and beetroot are shown at their best in simple dishes. So too are the many shades of green, characteristic of springtime, found in asparagus, broad beans, peas and fresh young spinach. May is the traditional month for English asparagus, although the exact weeks will depend on the weather. The same is true of broad beans and peas. A few warm weeks will also see British-grown watercress.

New potatoes now seem to be available all year round, but the exquisite Jersey Royals appear only in spring. Unfortunately, they are never cheap.

Purple-sprouting broccoli is a springtime speciality of British growers; look in local markets and farm shops. Also look out for spring cabbage varieties and (unhearted) spring greens.

If you have a good fishmonger, now is the time to buy crab, wild salmon and sea trout (also called salmon trout).

Spring cookery should exploit all the freshness of this abundant season, with minimum artifice.

SUMMER

During the hottest months of the year, seasonal produce and cooking retains the light touch and fresh feel of spring (think of the variety of salad leaves) but has the added punch of sun-ripened flavours and colours: juicy red tomatoes, cherries, strawberries, black-, red- and whitecurrants, golden and purple plums. Gooseberries appear early in the season, raspberries somewhat later. Imported peaches, nectarines and melons are at their prime.

The vegetables of the season are crisp and succulent – courgettes, broccoli, French and runner beans. Globe artichokes are likely to be imported from France. Corn on the cob appears in late summer.

Salads are full of flavour, colour and texture, with British-grown cucumber, celery, tomatoes and fresh raw beetroot.

Locally caught herrings, mackerel and squid join crab on the summer menu.

With a palette of nature's colours, tastes and textures before us, food shopping and cooking is an inexpensive and easy pleasure.

AUTUMN

The countryside seems to turn to gold as we reap the harvests of our fields, orchards and hedgerows, taking advantage of the last warm days for apple and blackberry picking. In autumn we get a choice of traditional apple varieties – don't miss them, as many appear in the shops for a very short season. Pears and several types of plum, including damsons, are also harvested now, as are walnuts and hazelnuts. Imports include luscious pomegranates and figs.

Mussels, clams, scallops and oysters come back into season and cod and plenty of other white fish are good-quality and easily available.

Late summer and early autumn see the arrival of sun-ripened aubergines and peppers; corn on the cob and courgettes continue to be good. Now is also the time to go hunting for wild mushrooms (never eat anything you are in the slightest doubt about). As autumn progresses, cauliflowers and leeks get better.

As the evenings draw in and the weather turns chilly, our thoughts turn to warming bowls of soup, and what better ingredient than autumn's great golden-orange prize, the pumpkin. Other winter squash come in all shapes and sizes, making autumn food buying and cooking just as adventurous as in the summer.

WINTER

The season's tasty and comforting root vegetables are perfect for rustling up casseroles and soups to keep out the cold. With so many different cooking methods – roasting, frying, stewing, mashing – they need never be boring. The variety is almost endless, and includes Jerusalem artichokes, parsnips, turnips, swedes, celeriac, scorzonera and salsify (a long, thin root, sometimes called vegetable oyster).

The brassica family provides the bright colours of Savoy and red cabbages, little Brussels sprouts and good-value curly kale.

Home-grown apples and pears should still be available at good prices. Traditional imports for the Christmas season include cranberries, chestnuts, brazil nuts, pineapples, lychees and a wide variety of citrus fruits.

At the fishmonger, good cheap mussels are joined by bargain sprats and skate.

Cabbages and root vegetables are also the perfect partners to winter's other speciality, game; it's not always expensive, so be ready to take advantage of bargains.

A FEW REMARKS ABOUT
MENU PLANNING

When thinking about what foods go well together, I often base menus around certain cuisines or styles of cooking (for example, Italian, French, Greek, Thai, Chinese or South American).

Once you understand the spirit of the dish or the style of cooking, feel free to improvise and make changes. Discovering new taste combinations is, for me, the most exciting and creative aspect of cooking.

Remember to plan your time sensibly. For most people, the first attempt at a dish may take twice as long as expected. Plan menus to include only one untried recipe or lengthy preparation, making the other courses a little easier.

Other aspects of menu planning may seem obvious, but it's worth taking a few minutes to make sure you have a variety of colours, flavours and textures. Choose accompanying salads, vegetables, sauces and garnishes to add contrast where needed.

Here are some menu suggestions using combinations of recipes featured in the book. Plan ahead, allow time to give them your best shot and enjoy them!

menu suggestions

ORIGINAL SUNDAY TIMES MENU
£1 for 4
Spicy Mexican Barbecue Bean Soup
Hot Dog Fusilli
Cinnamon Baked Apples 'en papillote'

ITALIAN VERVE
£4 for 4
Verdura Tonnato
Turkey Osso Buco
Coffee Risotto

SOUTH AMERICAN FEEL
£4 for 4
Ceviche of Whiting
Grilled Chicken Wings
  on Drunken Black Beans
  with Chilli Verde

ENGLISH FARE
£4 for 4
B.L.T. Salad
Soft Roe Potato Cakes
  with Caper Mayo
Apple Bread and Butter Pudding

GREEK FLAVOURS
£1 for 4
Avgolemono
  (Egg and Lemon Soup)
Lentil Moussaka Tart

SUMMER PICNIC
£3 for 4
Arrancini
Verdura Tonnato
Caraway, Onion and Bacon Tart

MEDITERRANEAN INSPIRED
£4 for 4
Sambusak
  (Cheese and Potato Pasties)
Cod Tagine

HOT AND COLD PASTA BUFFET
£3 for 4
Jumbled Pasta, Chickpea and
  Basil Salad
Spaghetti with Potatoes and Wilted
  Beans
Trenette with Tuna and Tomatoes

DINNER IN AN HOUR OR LESS
£4 for 4
Pesto Baked Mushrooms
Grey Mullet in Acqua Pazza
Prune and Almond Frittata

SUMMER EVENING BARBECUE
£4 for 4
Chargrilled Calamari Salad
Persian Koftas with Pitta Toasts
Shanghai Fishburgers
Barbecue Spice Rub Chicken

SOUPS

Pumpkin bisque

Pumpkins are often underrated, but their mellow flavour makes them incredibly versatile, ideal for both sweet and savoury dishes. It's certainly worth making the most of them when they appear in markets in the autumn.

Instead of the bread and garlic in this recipe, you could use six to eight pieces of garlic bread.

25 g (1 oz) butter
1 small onion, chopped
450 g (1 lb) peeled pumpkin, seeds removed,
  cut into chunks
375 ml (12 fl oz) milk
375 ml (12 fl oz) chicken or vegetable stock
3 slices of white bread
2 garlic cloves, halved
salt and freshly ground pepper
freshly grated nutmeg

Heat the butter in a heavy-bottomed saucepan, add the onion and cook until soft and translucent. Add the pumpkin and cook, stirring occasionally, for a further 5 minutes. Add the milk and stock and bring to the boil.

Meanwhile, lightly toast the bread, then rub with the cut cloves of garlic and cut each slice into four pieces. Add to the boiling soup and reduce the heat to a simmer. Cook for about 30 minutes or until the pumpkin is tender.

Pour into a liquidizer and blend to a fine, creamy-textured purée. If the soup is too thick you may need to add a little more milk. Season to taste with salt, pepper and nutmeg; serve hot.

Mussel chowder

Chowders are normally associated with clams, but I find them tough and tasteless – give me mussels any day. If you are feeling extravagant, add a pinch of saffron to the chowder with the milk and cream; its flavour goes beautifully with mussels.

900 g (2 lb) fresh mussels, scrubbed and debearded
15 g (½ oz) butter
50 g (2 oz) streaky bacon, cut into small pieces
1 onion, chopped
½ leek, cut into small dice
1 carrot, cut into small dice
1 garlic clove, crushed
225 g (8 oz) potatoes, cut into small dice
150 ml (¼ pint) milk
4 tablespoons single cream
1–2 tablespoons chopped fresh parsley
salt and freshly ground pepper

Place the mussels in a large saucepan, add 450 ml (¾ pint) water, cover with a tight-fitting lid and bring to the boil over a high heat. Cook for 2 minutes or until the mussels open. Drain them in a colander, retaining the cooking liquid. Remove the mussels from their shells; discard the shells.

Heat the butter in a heavy-bottomed saucepan, add the bacon, onion, leek, carrot and garlic and cook for 2 minutes or until the vegetables are tender. Strain the mussel cooking liquid and add to the pan, then add the potatoes. Bring to the boil, then reduce the heat and simmer until the potatoes are cooked.

Add the milk and cream, chopped parsley and mussels. Season to taste with pepper and salt if required; serve hot.

Roasted corn broth
with chunky pea guacamole

3 fresh or frozen corn on the cob
50 g (2 oz) butter, melted
salt and freshly ground pepper
750 ml (1¼ pints) chicken or vegetable stock
100 g (4 oz) cooked black beans
50 g (2 oz) Cheddar cheese, coarsely grated

For the pea guacamole:
100 g (4 oz) cooked peas
1 small green chilli, halved, deseeded and finely chopped
2 tomatoes, deseeded and cut into small pieces
2 tablespoons chopped fresh coriander
2 tablespoons shredded spring onions
1 teaspoon fresh lime juice
pinch of ground cumin

Preheat the oven to 200°C/400°F/Gas Mark 6.

Place the corn cobs on a baking sheet, brush with the butter, sprinkle with salt and pepper and cook until tender and lightly browned; this will take 20–25 minutes. Turn the cobs regularly so they brown evenly.

Remove from the oven and, when cool enough to handle, hold the cobs over a chopping board and use a knife to scrape off all the kernels; reserve the kernels. Cut the cobs into chunks and return to the oven to roast for a further 10 minutes.

Bring the stock to the boil in a saucepan, add the roasted cobs, reduce the heat and simmer for 40–45 minutes. Strain the corn broth through a sieve and season to taste.

To make the pea guacamole, mash the peas with a fork, add the remaining ingredients and season to taste.

To serve, divide the guacamole between four soup plates or bowls, add the reserved corn kernels and the black beans, then pour over the broth and top with the grated cheese; serve at once.

Avgolemono (Greek egg and lemon soup)

I discovered this soup while on holiday in Corfu. I loved its simplicity and tanginess and couldn't wait to try making it myself. Basmati rice, while not authentic, adds a lovely fragrance to the soup. I sometimes serve it lightly chilled.

1 litre (1¾ pints) chicken stock
50 g (2 oz) long-grain rice (preferably basmati)
2 eggs
2 tablespoons fresh lemon juice
salt and freshly ground pepper

Bring the stock to the boil in a saucepan, add the rice and simmer until the rice is cooked and tender, about 12 minutes.

Break the eggs into a bowl, add the lemon juice and whisk until light and frothy.

A little at a time, stir the cooked rice and hot liquid into the eggs, until all is blended together. Return to the pan and cook over a low heat, stirring all the time, until the soup thickens enough to coat the back of a spoon – it must not be allowed to boil. Season to taste with salt and pepper and serve at once. Alternatively, leave to cool, then chill.

Green tomato gazpacho

At the end of summer, gardeners often find they have
a glut of green tomatoes. This chilled soup is a great
way to use them up, and of course it is just as good
with red tomatoes. I like to serve gazpacho topped
with a spoonful of crème fraîche mixed with a little
shredded fresh basil.

2 slices of white bread, crusts removed
450 g (1 lb) green tomatoes, roughly chopped
1 green pepper, halved, deseeded and roughly chopped
½ cucumber, cut into chunks
½ onion, roughly chopped
1 garlic clove, crushed
½ teaspoon coriander seeds, crushed
5 tablespoons olive oil
4 tablespoons white wine vinegar
salt and freshly ground pepper
sugar

Place the bread in a small bowl and pour on about
600 ml (1 pint) cold water.

Place the tomatoes, pepper, cucumber, onion,
garlic and coriander in a liquidizer and blend to a
smooth purée. Strain the purée through a fine sieve
into a bowl.

Squeeze the water from the bread and place the
bread in the liquidizer. Blend to a pulp, then, with the
machine running, add the olive oil a little at a time
until incorporated into the bread. Add the vinegar, a
good pinch of salt and 4 tablespoons of the strained
tomato mixture and blend for a further 30 seconds.

Stir the bread mixture into the bowl of tomato
mixture. Adjust the consistency by adding a little
more water if necessary. Season to taste, adding a
pinch of sugar and more vinegar if required. Chill
the gazpacho until ready to serve.

Frozen broad bean and lemongrass vichyssoise

This variation on the classic, creamy, chilled vichyssoise has a subtle and delicate flavour; it is just as delicious made with peas instead of broad beans.

75 g (3 oz) butter
75 g (3 oz) leeks, roughly chopped
2 stalks of lemongrass, chopped
1/2 teaspoon fresh root ginger, chopped
1 litre (1³/₄ pints) chicken or vegetable stock
450 g (1 lb) frozen broad beans, shelled
250 ml (8 fl oz) milk
salt and freshly ground pepper
sugar
4 sprigs of mint, finely shredded

Heat the butter in a saucepan, add the leeks, lemongrass and ginger and cook over a low heat until soft. Add the stock, bring to the boil and simmer for 10 minutes. Add the shelled beans, return to the boil, then remove from the heat.

Pour into a liquidizer and blend to a purée. (For a really smooth soup, strain through a sieve.) Add the milk and season to taste with salt, pepper and a pinch of sugar. Chill until ready to serve. Sprinkle with the shredded mint just before serving.

Cabbage, turnip and black pudding soup

1 Savoy cabbage
2 large turnips
4 tablespoons olive oil
1 garlic clove, crushed
1 litre (1¾ pints) chicken stock
100 g (4 oz) black pudding, thinly sliced
salt and freshly ground black pepper

Remove and discard the outside leaves of the cabbage, then cut the cabbage into about 2.5 cm (1 inch) pieces. Peel the turnips and cut them in half, then into 5 mm (¼ inch) thick slices.

Heat half the oil in a large saucepan, add the garlic and cabbage and cook until the cabbage starts to soften. Add the sliced turnips, season lightly and cook for a further 2–3 minutes. Pour in the stock, bring to the boil, reduce the heat and simmer for 20–25 minutes or until the turnips are tender.

Add the black pudding, season to taste and simmer gently for a further 2 minutes. Serve hot, in bowls, drizzled with the remaining olive oil and sprinkled with some coarsely ground black pepper, accompanied by crusty baguette.

French onion soup with herring crostini

A classic warming soup with a fishy twist!

2 tablespoons olive oil
50 g (2 oz) butter
450 g (1 lb) onions, thinly sliced
2 teaspoons sugar
1 small garlic clove, crushed
1 tablespoon tomato purée
125 ml (4 fl oz) white wine
1 litre (1¾ pints) chicken stock

For the herring crostini:
200 g (7 oz) canned herrings in oil
salt and freshly ground pepper
1 small baguette
75 g (3 oz) Cheddar or Gruyère cheese, grated

Heat the oil and butter in a large saucepan, add the onions and sauté until tender. Sprinkle with the sugar and continue to cook until the sugar caramelizes and the onions turn a beautiful dark brown.

Add the garlic and tomato purée and cook, stirring once or twice, for a further 5 minutes. Pour in the wine and stock, bring to the boil, reduce the heat and simmer for 30–35 minutes.

To make the herring crostini, mash the herrings in a bowl and season lightly. Cut the baguette into eight 1 cm (½ inch) slices, toast them and spread with the mashed herring. Keep warm. Preheat the grill to its highest setting.

Pour the hot soup into heatproof bowls, top each with two herring crostini and sprinkle with the cheese. Place the bowls under the hot grill until the cheese is brown and bubbling. Serve at once.

Tourin blanchi (Garlic soup)

This delicious rich garlic soup has only one drawback – its lingering flavour. It is perhaps best reserved for close friends and consenting adults!

1 tablespoon olive oil
1 large onion, thinly sliced
1 whole head of garlic, cut into cloves, peeled and
  thinly sliced
25 g (1 oz) plain flour
750 ml (1¼ pints) chicken stock
2 eggs
1 teaspoon white wine vinegar
salt and freshly ground pepper

Heat the oil in a heavy-bottomed saucepan, add the onion and garlic and cook over a low heat until soft. Stir in the flour and continue to cook over a low heat, stirring frequently, for 1 minute to allow the flour to cook.

Add the stock a little at a time, stirring well until all is incorporated. Bring to the boil, reduce the heat and simmer gently for 30 minutes.

Pour into a liquidizer and blend to a smooth purée.

Separate the eggs, beat the yolks with the vinegar and whisk the whites lightly.

When ready to serve, return the puréed soup to the boil, then remove from the heat. Gradually beat in the egg whites, then the yolks, season to taste and serve at once (on no account allow the soup to boil after the eggs have been added).

Spicy Mexican barbecue bean soup

A last-minute garnish of diced crisp bacon goes well with this soup.

2 tablespoons olive oil
1 onion, chopped
1/4 teaspoon dried chilli flakes
1 potato, cut into small pieces
400 g (14 oz) canned baked beans in tomato sauce
300 ml (1/2 pint) chicken or vegetable stock
1 tablespoon brown sugar
1 teaspoon mustard
1 tablespoon molasses (optional)
salt and freshly ground pepper

Heat the oil in a saucepan, add the onion and cook until soft. Add the chilli flakes and cook for about 1 minute to release the flavour, then add the potato and most of the beans (reserve 4 tablespoons for garnishing the soup). Stir well, add the stock and cook over a low heat for 15–20 minutes or until the potato is nearly tender.

Combine the sugar, mustard, molasses, salt and pepper. Add to the soup and cook for a further 5 minutes.

Pour into a liquidizer and blend to a smooth purée. Taste and adjust the seasoning if required. Serve hot, garnished with the reserved beans.

Thai chicken broth

750 ml (1¼ pints) chicken stock
16 marinated Thai chicken wings (page 37)
200 g (7 oz) canned tomatoes, drained and chopped
½ teaspoon shredded fresh root ginger
100 g (4 oz) button mushrooms, sliced
50 g (2 oz) Chinese cabbage, shredded
4 spring onions, finely chopped
2 tablespoons light soy sauce
pinch of dried chilli flakes
2 tablespoons fresh coriander leaves

Put the stock in a large saucepan and bring to a simmer.
Add the chicken wings, tomatoes and ginger and
poach very gently for 15–20 minutes or until the
wings are cooked. Remove the wings and keep warm.

Skim off any impurities that have risen to the
surface of the stock, add the mushrooms, cabbage
and spring onions and simmer for 2 minutes.

Stir in the soy sauce, chilli flakes and coriander,
taste and adjust the seasoning if required. Divide the
chicken wings between four soup plates or bowls,
ladle on the soup and serve hot.

Stinging nettle callaloo with crispy lardons

A variation on a soup from the Caribbean. Callaloo, also known as Caribbean cabbage, is an ear-shaped leaf plant similar to spinach. Here, nettles make a very cheap alternative, but don't forget to wear gloves when you pick them. Spinach can be used in this recipe if you prefer.

675 g (1½ lb) young stinging nettle leaves
2 tablespoons sunflower oil
1 onion, chopped
1 garlic clove, crushed
pinch of cayenne pepper
1 tablespoon plain flour
600 ml (1 pint) chicken stock
50 g (2 oz) fresh parsley
1 teaspoon fresh thyme leaves
salt and freshly ground black pepper
4 rashers of streaky bacon, cut into small strips

Wash the nettles thoroughly, drain and chop them roughly. Heat half the oil in a heavy-bottomed saucepan, add the onion, garlic and cayenne, and fry until lightly golden. Add the nettles and cook over a low heat for 3–4 minutes. Add the flour and blend well with the nettles. Pour on the stock, a little at a time, stirring constantly. Cook over a low heat for 10–15 minutes.

Add the parsley and thyme, then pour into a liquidizer and blend to a smooth purée. Taste and adjust the seasoning.

Heat the remaining oil in a small frying pan, add the strips of bacon and fry until crisp.

Serve the soup hot, topped with the crispy lardons.

Dal soup with toasted cumin and rocket oil

Lentils and cumin are a marriage made in heaven, their earthy, nutty flavours complementing each other perfectly. The rocket adds a peppery touch.

1 litre (1¾ pints) chicken or vegetable stock
1 teaspoon cumin seeds, toasted and ground
½ teaspoon ground coriander
⅛ teaspoon cayenne pepper
1 small bay leaf
225 g (8 oz) lentils, rinsed
2 tablespoons olive oil
1 carrot, chopped
½ onion, chopped
salt and freshly ground pepper

For the rocket oil:
1 tablespoon fresh lemon juice
3 tablespoons olive oil
50 g (2 oz) rocket

Bring the stock to the boil in a saucepan, add the toasted cumin, coriander, cayenne and bay leaf. Add the lentils, reduce the heat and simmer until tender, about 50 minutes.

Heat the oil in a small saucepan, add the carrot and onion and cook over a low heat until soft.

Add this mixture to the simmering lentils and cook for a further 10–15 minutes.

To make the rocket oil, place the lemon juice, olive oil and rocket in a liquidizer together with a little salt and pepper and blend just long enough to form a coarse purée.

Remove the bay leaf from the soup, then pour into a liquidizer and blend to a coarse purée. Divide the soup between four soup plates or bowls, top each with a spoonful of the rocket oil and serve hot. Toasted croûtons are a good addition.

STARTERS
AND **SALADS**

Pesto baked mushrooms

This stuffing can also be used for tomatoes, courgettes, aubergines or onions, although they will take longer to cook (8–10 minutes for tomatoes, 15–20 minutes for courgettes and 45–55 minutes for aubergines and onions).

450 g (1 lb) large button mushrooms
3 tablespoons olive oil
1 onion, chopped
2 courgettes, chopped
1 small jar of pesto sauce, about 125 ml (4 fl oz)
25–50 g (1–2 oz) Parmesan cheese, grated
1 egg yolk
salt and freshly ground pepper

Gently pull out the stalks from the mushrooms and chop the stalks finely. Heat half the oil in a frying pan, add the chopped onion, courgettes and mushroom stalks and cook over a low heat until soft, about 5 minutes. Leave until cold.

Preheat the oven to 200°C/400°F/Gas Mark 6.

Place the onion mixture in a liquidizer with the pesto sauce and blend to a coarse purée. Add enough Parmesan to form a thick paste. Transfer to a bowl and stir in the egg yolk. Taste and adjust the seasoning.

Lightly fry the mushroom caps in the remaining oil for 1 minute, then drain. Fill each cap with the pesto stuffing, place on a baking sheet and bake for 5–8 minutes or until tender when tested with a small sharp knife. Alternatively, cook the mushrooms under a hot grill. Serve hot.

Oriental mushroom fritters with peanut curry dip

vegetable oil for deep-frying
450 g (1 lb) button mushrooms
2 tablespoons five-spice powder
1/2 teaspoon dried chilli flakes
150 g (5 oz) cornflour
1/2 teaspoon baking powder
salt and freshly ground black pepper
1 egg white

For the peanut curry dip:
150 ml (1/4 pint) chicken or vegetable stock
1/2 teaspoon curry powder
1/2 garlic clove, crushed
1/2 teaspoon honey
2 tablespoons peanut butter
1/2 teaspoon light soy sauce
dash of wine vinegar

Heat 2 tablespoons of the oil in a frying pan and fry the mushrooms for 2 minutes or until they begin to soften. Season with five-spice powder and chilli flakes, transfer to a bowl and leave until cold.

To make the peanut curry dip, place all the ingredients in a saucepan and bring to the boil; simmer gently for 3–4 minutes, then leave to cool.

Place the cornflour and baking powder in a bowl with 125 ml (4 fl oz) iced water, 3 tablespoons of the oil and a little salt and pepper and mix until smooth. When you are ready to fry the mushrooms, whisk the egg white until stiff, then fold into the batter.

Heat the oil for deep-frying to 180°C/350°F (until a cube of bread browns in 30 seconds). Dip the mushrooms in the batter, then into the hot oil and fry until golden, 1–2 minutes. Drain well and serve with the peanut dip.

Baked tomatoes with coddled eggs

4 large beefsteak tomatoes
salt and freshly ground pepper
4 eggs
40 g (1½ oz) butter

Preheat the oven to 160°C/325°F/Gas Mark 3.

Slice the tops off the tomatoes and scoop out the cores, seeds and juice. Sprinkle a little salt and pepper inside the tomato shells, then place them in a lightly buttered ovenproof dish.

Break each egg into a cup, then slide into the tomato shells. Place a little knob of butter on each egg and season with a little more salt and pepper.

Bake the tomatoes for 12–15 minutes or until the egg whites are firm but the yolks are still soft.

Serve hot, topped with a spoonful of tapenade, pesto or chilli verde (page 90).

Thai chicken wings in spiced coconut milk

For the best results, marinate the chicken wings for at least 6 hours before you cook them.

1 teaspoon curry paste
1 small garlic clove, crushed
¼ teaspoon dried chilli flakes
½ teaspoon ground coriander
½ teaspoon turmeric
salt and freshly ground pepper
sugar
250 ml (8 fl oz) coconut milk
3 tablespoons vegetable oil
20 fresh chicken wings, boned

Place the curry paste, garlic, chilli, spices, salt, pepper and a pinch of sugar in a bowl, add the coconut milk and oil and whisk together. Add the chicken wings and turn to coat them in the marinade. Cover and place in the refrigerator for up to 24 hours.

To serve, soak four or more bamboo skewers in cold water for 30 minutes. Preheat the grill or barbecue. Remove the chicken wings from the marinade and thread them on to the soaked skewers. Grill or barbecue until cooked and golden, turning occasionally; about 5–8 minutes.

I like to serve them with basmati rice, a crisp salad and a dip made from 100 g (4 oz) mayonnaise mixed with 2 tablespoons chopped mango chutney. They are also very good on their own, as cocktail nibbles, or you can use them in the Thai chicken broth (page 28).

Caraway, onion and bacon tart

2 tablespoons butter
4 rashers of streaky bacon, diced
4 onions, thinly sliced
2 teaspoons caraway seeds
salt and freshly ground pepper
2 eggs
2 egg yolks
300 ml (½ pint) double cream

For the pastry:
275 g (10 oz) plain flour
pinch of salt
150 g (5 oz) cold butter or margarine, diced

To make the pastry, sift the flour and salt into a
bowl and rub in the butter or margarine until the
mixture resembles fine breadcrumbs. Add just enough
water to bind, then leave to rest in the refrigerator
for 30 minutes before using.

Preheat the oven to 200°C/400°F/Gas Mark 6.

Roll out the pastry and use to line a 22 cm
(9 inch) buttered flan tin. Prick the base evenly with
a fork, line it with greaseproof paper, fill it with
baking beans and bake blind for 6–8 minutes.
Remove the paper and beans and return the pastry
case to the oven for a further 5 minutes or until
cooked and lightly golden, then leave to cool.

Heat the butter in a frying pan, add the diced
bacon and cook until crisp. Remove the bacon, add
the onions and caraway seeds to the pan with a little
salt and pepper and cook over a low heat until
golden and tender, then leave to cool slightly.

Arrange the onions and bacon in the pastry case.
Beat the eggs and yolks with the cream and a little salt
and pepper, pour over the onions and bacon and bake
for 30 minutes or until golden and set. Serve warm.

White bean hummus with yoghurt

An alternative to the usual hummus made with chickpeas. Chill overnight to allow the flavours to blend and develop.

400 g (14 oz) canned cannellini beans
2 garlic cloves, crushed
2 tablespoons tahini (sesame seed paste)
juice of 1 lemon
½ teaspoon ground cumin
3 tablespoons olive oil
2 tablespoons natural yoghurt
salt
1 tablespoon chopped fresh parsley

Drain the cannellini beans and place them in a liquidizer or food processor with the remaining ingredients, except the parsley. Blend to a smooth paste. Taste and add more salt, garlic or lemon juice if required. Refrigerate overnight.

To serve, sprinkle with the parsley and drizzle with a little olive oil. I sometimes add a further garnish of chopped black olives and diced tomatoes.

Mexican dirty rice salad

A substantial salad that can equally well be served
as a vegetarian main course, especially with plenty of
Mexican garnishes: diced avocado and tomato, sour
cream and coarsely grated Cheddar cheese.

50 g (2 oz) butter
225 g (8 oz) long-grain rice
1 green chilli, deseeded and chopped
1 teaspoon ground cumin
500 ml (16 fl oz) vegetable stock
salt and freshly ground pepper
400 g (14 oz) canned black beans
4 spring onions, shredded
2 tablespoons chopped fresh coriander

For the dressing:
5 tablespoons vegetable oil
1½ tablespoons white wine vinegar
1 teaspoon mustard

Heat the butter in a wide saucepan over a low heat,
add the rice and cook, stirring, until opaque. Add
the chilli and cumin, stir well and cook for a further
1 minute.

Bring the stock to the boil, add to the rice with
1 teaspoon salt and bring back to the boil. Reduce
the heat, cover with a tight-fitting lid and cook for
20 minutes or until the rice is tender.

Drain the rice and transfer to a large bowl.
Add the black beans, shredded spring onions and
coriander and mix well. Leave to cool slightly.

Place the dressing ingredients in a bowl and
whisk together, then pour over the rice salad and
serve at room temperature.

Crispy Malaysian vegetable salad

150 g (5 oz) broccoli, cut into small florets
2 carrots, cut into matchsticks
1/2 red pepper, deseeded and cut into matchsticks
1/2 yellow pepper, deseeded and cut into matchsticks
1/2 cucumber, cut into matchsticks
50 g (2 oz) beansprouts
4 spring onions, shredded
1/2 bunch of watercress
2 tablespoons roasted peanuts

For the dressing:
3 tablespoons lime juice
1 tablespoon chopped fresh mint
1 tablespoon chopped fresh coriander
pinch of dried chilli flakes
2 tablespoons light soy sauce
2 tablespoons sugar
6 tablespoons vegetable oil

Place all the dressing ingredients in a bowl and whisk together. This can be made up to 2 days ahead and kept in the refrigerator.

Blanch the broccoli in boiling salted water until just tender but retaining a little crunchiness. Rinse under cold water, drain and dry on paper towels.

Place all the vegetables in a bowl, add the watercress and the dressing, mix well and leave for up to 15 minutes before serving, sprinkled with the roasted peanuts.

Jumbled pasta, chickpea and basil salad

This salad is a great way to use up those odd packets of pasta that are never quite enough to make a dish on their own. For a real treat, top the pasta salad with some freshly grated pecorino cheese.

150 g (5 oz) dried chickpeas or 275 g (10 oz) canned chickpeas
225 g (8 oz) mixed dried pasta
2 ripe tomatoes, deseeded and chopped
50 g (2 oz) fresh or frozen broad beans, cooked
½ onion, thinly sliced
3 tablespoons chopped fresh basil or parsley

For the dressing:
4 tablespoons olive oil
½ garlic clove, crushed
1 tablespoon red wine vinegar
¼ teaspoon dried chilli flakes
salt and freshly ground pepper

If using dried chickpeas, soak them overnight in plenty of cold water. The next day, drain them well, place in a saucepan, cover with fresh cold water and bring to the boil (do not add salt otherwise the chickpeas will harden and will be difficult to cook). Reduce the heat and simmer for about 1½ hours or until tender. When cooked, drain well and place in a bowl.

Cook the pasta in boiling salted water to which a little oil has been added to prevent the pasta from sticking together. When the pasta is cooked al dente (just tender, but still firm to the bite), drain well and add to the chickpeas.

While the pasta and chickpeas are still warm, place all the dressing ingredients in a bowl and whisk together. Pour over the pasta and chickpeas and leave to cool.

Just before serving, add the chopped tomatoes, broad beans, onion and herbs. For the best results serve at room temperature, not chilled.

Verdura tonnato

Here the classic tonnato (tuna) sauce, which usually accompanies cold poached veal, is served as a dip for a selection of crisp raw vegetables.

200 g (7 oz) canned tuna, drained
1 teaspoon anchovy essence
1 teaspoon capers, drained
2 tablespoons fresh lemon juice
salt and freshly ground pepper
150 g (5 oz) mayonnaise

Place the tuna, anchovy essence and capers in a liquidizer and blend to a smooth paste. Add the lemon juice, salt and pepper and transfer to a bowl. Add the mayonnaise and beat with the tuna mixture. Add a little water if it is too thick. Serve with vegetable crudités (carrots, green beans, cucumber, celeriac).

Salad of sardines 'Monégasque'

The name comes from a Provençal word for Monaco, and this salad is full of the distinctive ingredients of the south of France; whenever I prepare it I dream of travelling through Provence, stopping for a light lunch and a glass of wine.

175 g (6 oz) new potatoes
100 g (4 oz) dried penne pasta
2 tomatoes, cut into quarters
2 hard-boiled eggs, shelled
½ small onion, cut into rings
4 red radishes
1 teaspoon capers, drained
200 g (7 oz) canned sardines

For the dressing:
2 teaspoons white wine vinegar
6 teaspoons olive oil
½ teaspoon anchovy essence
½ garlic clove, crushed
salt and freshly ground pepper

Boil the potatoes in salted water. At the same time cook the pasta in plenty of boiling salted water, to which a little oil has been added to prevent the pasta from sticking together.

When the potatoes are tender, drain, peel and slice them into a bowl. When the pasta is cooked al dente (just tender, but still firm to the bite), drain in a colander and add to the potatoes. Add the tomatoes, eggs, onion rings, radishes and capers and toss gently.

Drain the sardines, reserving the oil. Place the dressing ingredients in a bowl and whisk together with the sardine oil. Season to taste, then add to the salad and toss gently to mix.

Serve the salad on a serving platter, topped with the sardines. I like to garnish this dish with crunchy deep-fried parsley.

B.L.T. salad
(Bacon, liver and tomato salad)

My version of the infamous B.L.T. (normally a sandwich made with bacon, lettuce and tomatoes). My ingredients are bacon, chicken livers and tomatoes, transformed into a delicious warm salad.

6 tablespoons olive oil
400 g (14 oz) fresh chicken livers, cleaned and halved
½ teaspoon ground cumin
6 tomatoes, halved
4 rashers of streaky bacon
2 tablespoons roughly chopped fresh coriander leaves
6 tablespoons balsamic vinegar
mixed salad leaves

Heat half the oil in a frying pan until very hot, add the chicken livers, seasoned with a little cumin, and cook for 2–3 minutes, stirring occasionally, until brown and crisp on the outside, yet still pink and tender inside.

Preheat the grill. Brush the tomatoes with a little olive oil. Grill the bacon and tomatoes until the bacon is crisp and the tomatoes are soft but not mushy. Sprinkle the tomatoes with some of the coriander and keep the bacon and tomatoes warm.

Remove the livers from the frying pan and keep warm. Add the vinegar to the pan and bring to the boil. Whisk in the remaining olive oil.

Toss the salad leaves with some of the warm dressing and arrange on four plates. Crumble the crispy bacon over the leaves and place three tomato halves on each plate. Top with the chicken livers and drizzle the remaining dressing over the livers. Garnish with the remaining coriander leaves.

Chargrilled calamari salad

However you cook them, squid need a very short cooking time, otherwise they will toughen. If you want to
cook them on the barbecue, leave them whole and cut
them into rings when cooked. If you prefer your squid
to be crispy, dip the rings in breadcrumbs and deep-fry
until golden. There are several good brands of frozen
squid (calamari) at very reasonable prices.

4 tomatoes, cut into quarters
6 black olives, pitted and halved
1 red onion, halved and thinly sliced
1 tablespoon fresh oregano leaves
600 g (1¼ lb) squid, cleaned and cut into 5 mm (¼ inch) rings
salt and freshly ground pepper
2 Little Gem lettuces, or other crisp lettuce leaves

For the sauce:
2 garlic cloves, crushed
4 tablespoons olive oil
4 tablespoons vegetable oil
1 egg
1 tablespoon white wine vinegar
dash of Worcestershire sauce
dash of Tabasco sauce

To make the sauce, whisk all the ingredients together
in a bowl or blend in a liquidizer.

Toss the tomatoes, olives, onion and oregano
together with just enough of the sauce to coat lightly.

Sprinkle the squid with a little salt and pepper
and grill for 1 minute under a hot grill or in a cast-
iron grill pan.

Arrange the lettuce leaves on four plates, top with
the tomato salad, then the grilled squid; serve warm.

Italian tuna and white bean salad

A delicious combination of hot and cold, this makes an excellent first course either on its own or as part of a selection of mixed antipasti.

400 g (14 oz) canned cannellini beans
1 onion, finely chopped
1 garlic clove, finely chopped
1 teaspoon dried or fresh oregano
200 g (7 oz) canned tuna in oil, drained and flaked,
    reserving the oil
6 tablespoons olive oil
2 tablespoons white wine vinegar
salt and freshly ground pepper
4 ripe plum tomatoes
1 tablespoon fresh chopped basil (optional)

Heat the beans and their liquid in a small saucepan, then drain and rinse in boiling water. Place in a bowl, add the onion, garlic and oregano. Stir, then add the reserved tuna oil, olive oil and vinegar and mix well together. Add the tuna and season to taste.

Slice the tomatoes 1 cm (1/2 inch) thick and arrange on a shallow serving dish. Season with salt, pepper and a little olive oil. Arrange the beans and tuna on top and sprinkle with the fresh basil.

Ceviche of whiting

In some parts of South America ceviche is made with oranges instead of limes.

450 g (1 lb) very fresh whiting fillet
juice of 2 limes
salt
1 tablespoon coriander seeds, crushed
4 tablespoons olive oil
½ tablespoon tomato ketchup
dash of Tabasco sauce
1 small onion, finely sliced
2 tomatoes, skinned, deseeded and cut into small dice
50 g (2 oz) cucumber, peeled and cut into small dice
1 tablespoon chopped fresh coriander, plus extra to garnish
corn tortillas, fried until crisp

Cut the fish into 2 cm (¾ inch) cubes and place in a bowl. Pour on the lime juice and a little salt and toss well to coat the fish. Cover the bowl and place it in the refrigerator for up to 5 hours, stirring from time to time. The fish will become opaque.

Drain off the juice and combine some of it (according to taste – you may not need all of it) with the crushed coriander seeds, oil, ketchup and Tabasco to form a dressing. Pour the dressing over the fish and gently stir in the onion, tomatoes, cucumber and fresh coriander. Refrigerate for a further 1 hour.

Serve chilled, layered between the tortilla crisps. Garnish with fresh coriander.

Arrancini

Arrancini is the Italian term for small oranges; these
look-alikes are made of red salmon bound with cooked
rice and fried until crisp. The traditional accompaniment is a well-flavoured tomato sauce. Tartare sauce
or a pesto-flavoured mayonnaise are also good.

200 g (7 oz) arborio rice
1 hard-boiled egg, chopped
200 g (7 oz) canned red salmon, drained and flaked
1 teaspoon chopped fresh parsley
½ teaspoon dried or fresh oregano
salt and freshly ground pepper
1 egg, beaten
150 g (5 oz) fresh white breadcrumbs
vegetable oil for deep-frying
lemon wedges, to serve

Cook the rice in plenty of salted boiling water for
12–15 minutes or until just tender. Drain well and
leave to dry for at least 30 minutes. (The rice can be
cooked up to a day ahead and kept in the refrigerator.)

Place the cooked rice in a bowl, add the chopped
hard-boiled egg, the flaked salmon, herbs, salt and
pepper. Place in the refrigerator for 1 hour.

Shape the chilled mixture into tiny balls, about
4 cm (1½ inches) in diameter. Place the beaten egg
in a saucer and the breadcrumbs on a plate. Roll
the rice balls first in the beaten egg, then in the
breadcrumbs, to coat evenly.

Heat the oil for deep-frying to 180°C/350°F
(until a cube of bread browns in 30 seconds). Fry the
rice balls for 3–4 minutes or until golden. Drain on
paper towels and serve with lemon wedges.

Beetroot 'gravad mackerel'

Mackerel makes an interesting variation on the classic
Scandinavian gravadlax (marinated salmon). Beetroot
has a sweet taste that goes well with the sweet dill
and mustard sauce.

2 tablespoons sugar
3 tablespoons salt
a little freshly ground pepper
4 large, very fresh mackerel, cleaned and filleted
5 tablespoons chopped fresh dill, plus extra to garnish
1 cooked fresh beetroot (not in vinegar), coarsely grated
1 tablespoon capers (optional), to garnish
lemon wedges, to serve

For the dill and mustard sauce:
2 tablespoons mustard
2 teaspoons brown sugar
1 tablespoon white wine vinegar
4 tablespoons olive oil
2 tablespoons chopped fresh dill

Mix the sugar, salt and pepper together in a bowl.
Lay the mackerel fillets out flat, skin side down, and
sprinkle with the sugar and salt mixture. Cover each
fillet with some of the chopped dill. Arrange the fillets
head to tail in a shallow dish, just large enough to
hold the fish. Sprinkle with the remaining dill, then
cover with clingfilm and press down with a weighted
board, about 1–1.5 kg (2–3 lb). Leave in the refrigerator for 8 hours.

Sprinkle the grated beetroot over the fish and
return to the refrigerator for a further 8 hours.

To make the sauce, mix the mustard, brown
sugar and vinegar together in a bowl, whisk in the
oil, add the dill and season to taste.

To serve, scrape the dill mixture and beetroot from the fish and, using a long, sharp knife, cut the fillets into thin slices, beginning at the tail end.

Garnish with fresh dill and capers, if using. Serve with lemon wedges and serve the sauce separately.

Soft roe potato cakes with caper mayo

225 g (8 oz) soft herring roes, cleaned
75 ml (3 fl oz) milk
40 g (1½ oz) butter, softened
1 onion, finely chopped
275 g (10 oz) cooked mashed potatoes
1 tablespoon chopped fresh parsley
salt and freshly ground pepper
freshly grated nutmeg
2 large potatoes
3–4 tablespoons plain flour
2 eggs, beaten
vegetable oil for frying

For the caper mayo:
100 g (4 oz) mayonnaise
1 tablespoon chopped capers
juice and grated zest of 1 lemon

Poach the roes in the milk for 6–8 minutes, then drain, discarding the milk, and leave to cool.

Heat half the butter in a frying pan, add the onion and cook until golden. Place the mashed potatoes in a bowl, add the onion and beat in the remaining butter until smooth. Dice the cooked roes and gently stir into the potatoes, together with the parsley. Season to taste with salt, pepper and nutmeg. Place in the refrigerator for 1 hour.

Mix the ingredients for the caper mayonnaise in a small bowl.

Peel and grate the potatoes, and dry them in a clean tea towel. Divide the mashed potato mixture into eight pieces, then shape into ovals. Dip the potato cakes into the flour to coat lightly, then coat them with the beaten eggs, then finally coat them evenly with the grated potatoes.

Heat the oil in a frying pan and cook the potato cakes until golden and crisp on both sides, about 3–4 minutes. Drain on paper towels and serve hot, with the caper mayonnaise.

Roes on toast

Soft roes, for me, are one of our greatest treasures at a budget price, but unfortunately they are seldom used. Try them simply on toast, for breakfast or brunch, and you will discover just what you have been missing. Malt vinegar is the traditional dressing.

50 g (2 oz) butter
400 g (14 oz) soft herring roes, cleaned
salt and freshly ground black pepper
4 slices of white bread
2 tablespoons malt vinegar

Heat the butter in a frying pan, season the roes with salt and pepper and fry them until they begin to curl up and turn golden, about 1–2 minutes.

Meanwhile, toast the bread.

Arrange the roes on the toast and serve at once, sprinkled with the vinegar and a generous amount of black pepper.

Grilled stuffed mussels with pico de gallo

Pico de gallo means 'chicken's beak' in Spanish, and is the name given to a piquant salsa. You could add more Tabasco sauce to heighten the flavour, but take care not to overwhelm the mussels.

900 g (2 lb) fresh mussels, scrubbed and debearded
5 tablespoons white wine
25 g (1 oz) fresh white breadcrumbs
salt and freshly ground pepper

For the pico de gallo:
200 g (7 oz) canned tomatoes, drained and finely chopped
½ onion
½ garlic clove, crushed
½ teaspoon coriander seeds, crushed
1 tablespoon fresh coriander
2 tablespoons lime juice
1 tablespoon maple syrup
5 tablespoons olive oil
2 drops of Tabasco sauce

Place the mussels in a frying pan or a fairly shallow saucepan. Add the white wine and 125 ml (4 fl oz) water, cover with a tight-fitting lid and place over a high heat until the shells open, about 2–3 minutes. Drain the mussels in a colander, strain the cooking liquid and set aside.

Make the pico de gallo by placing all the ingredients in a liquidizer or food processor and blending together. Pour the mixture into a bowl, add the breadcrumbs and season lightly.

Remove the mussels from their shells and discard the shells that have the inner muscle attached. Arrange the mussels in their half shells on a baking sheet.

Preheat the grill. Place a little of the pico de gallo stuffing on each mussel half and cook under the hot grill until golden and crisp.

Place a little of the reserved mussel cooking liquid in the bottom of each serving bowl and top with the grilled mussels; serve at once.

Thai mussels

Mussels are often served as a first course in restaurants, but because they are quite fiddly to eat, they are very filling, and can easily become the main event.

900 g (2 lb) fresh mussels, scrubbed and debearded
2 tablespoons vegetable oil
½ onion, finely chopped
2 fresh red chillies, deseeded and finely chopped
  (or ½ teaspoon dried chilli flakes)
2 small garlic cloves, crushed
½ tablespoon brown sugar
1 tablespoon light soy sauce
2 tablespoons roughly chopped fresh mint
freshly ground black pepper

Place the mussels in a frying pan or a fairly shallow saucepan. Pour over 150 ml (¼ pint) water, cover with a tight-fitting lid and place over a high heat until the shells open, about 2–3 minutes. Transfer the mussels to a serving dish.

Heat the oil in the cleaned frying pan, add the onion, chillies, garlic, sugar and soy sauce and cook until tender. Pour the mixture over the mussels, sprinkle with the chopped mint and pepper and serve at once.

Tatin of sardines

450 g (1 lb) puff pastry
25 g (1 oz) butter
2 onions, thinly sliced
3 anchovy fillets, finely chopped
600 g (1¼ lb) fresh sardines, filleted, central bones removed
salt and freshly ground pepper
100 ml (3½ fl oz) olive oil
½ garlic clove, crushed
½ teaspoon coriander seeds, crushed
3 tomatoes, deseeded and diced
juice of ½ lemon

Preheat the oven to 200°C/400°F/Gas Mark 6.

Roll out the pastry on a lightly floured board to approximately 5 mm (¼ inch) thick. Using a 10 cm (4 inch) round cutter, cut out four pastry circles, prick each thoroughly with a fork and bake for 8–10 minutes or until cooked and golden. Remove from the oven and leave to cool.

Meanwhile, heat the butter in a saucepan, add the sliced onions and cook gently until golden, then add the chopped anchovies. Spread each baked tart with the onion and anchovy mixture. Arrange the sardine fillets on top. Season and brush with a little of the olive oil. Place in a hot oven for 5–6 minutes or until the sardines are cooked and lightly browned.

While the tarts are cooking, prepare a light sauce: heat the remaining oil in a saucepan, add the garlic and coriander seeds and heat gently. Add the diced tomatoes, lemon juice and salt and pepper and warm through to soften the tomatoes. Pour the sauce around the tarts and serve hot.

Caveached sardines on horseradish mash

For the best results, marinate the sardines for up to two days.

675 g (1½ lb) fresh sardines, filleted and cleaned
1 teaspoon salt
6 tablespoons olive oil
250 ml (8 fl oz) red wine vinegar
2 red onions, thinly sliced
2 garlic cloves, crushed
1 green chilli
1 bay leaf
¼ teaspoon black peppercorns

For the horseradish mash:
275 g (10 oz) new potatoes, peeled
2 tablespoons olive oil
1 teaspoon freshly grated horseradish
freshly ground pepper

Season the sardines with the salt. Heat 4 tablespoons of the oil in a frying pan and fry the sardines until lightly golden on both sides. Transfer them to a shallow dish and set aside.

In a saucepan, boil the vinegar, onions, garlic, chilli, bay leaf and peppercorns for 10 minutes, until the onions are tender. Remove from the heat and leave to cool. Add the remaining 2 tablespoons of oil and pour the liquid over the fish. Cover and place in the refrigerator for up to two days.

For the horseradish mash: boil the potatoes in lightly salted water until tender, drain, then purée through a fine sieve. Stir in the olive oil and horseradish and season to taste.

Place a little horseradish mash on each serving plate and top with the soused sardines, drizzled with some of their marinade.

Asian spiced herrings with fruit raita

1 teaspoon dried chilli flakes
½ garlic clove, crushed
1 teaspoon ground ginger
1 teaspoon garam masala
salt and freshly ground black pepper
6 tablespoons vegetable or olive oil
450 g (1 lb) fresh herrings, cleaned and cut into 5 cm
   (2 inch) pieces

For the raita sauce:
150 ml (¼ pint) natural yoghurt
½ teaspoon ground cumin
2 teaspoons chopped fresh coriander or mint
1 firm banana

In a shallow dish, mix together the chilli, garlic, ginger, garam masala, salt and pepper. Add 2 table-spoons of the oil and mix to a paste. Add the fish pieces and leave to marinate for 30 minutes.

To make the raita, mix together the yoghurt, cumin and coriander or mint in a bowl. Coarsely grate the banana into the yoghurt, stir gently to mix and season to taste.

Heat the remaining 4 tablespoons oil in a frying pan and fry the herring pieces until golden, about 4 minutes on each side. Drain on paper towels and serve hot, accompanied by the raita.

Mussel chowder, p. 19

Tatin of sardines, p. 56

Fettuccine with charred tomatoes and rosemary oil, p. 63

Kedgeree in filo purses, p. 79

Braised chicken with anchovies and olives, p. 89

Savoy cabbage and parsnip jalousie, p. 120

Baked plums in red wine syrup, p. 125

Prune and almond frittata, p. 132

Oatmeal fried herrings

If you like, you can serve these herrings with a
tartare sauce.

4 large herrings, cleaned and filleted
1 tablespoon herb-flavoured mustard
150 g (5 oz) butter
150 g (5 oz) fine oatmeal
salt and freshly ground pepper
2–3 tablespoons vegetable oil
1 tablespoon chopped fresh parsley
1 tablespoon capers
juice of ½ lemon

Lightly brush the herrings with the mustard. Melt
100 g (4 oz) of the butter and pour into a shallow
dish; season the oatmeal and place in another dish.
Dip the herrings into the melted butter and then into
the seasoned oatmeal, to coat evenly. Heat the oil in
a frying pan and fry the herrings until golden on
both sides. Transfer to a serving dish.

Heat the remaining butter in a frying pan until it
begins to foam and gives off a nutty aroma, add the
parsley, capers and lemon juice and pour over the
herrings. Serve at once.

PASTA
AND CO

Penne with caramelized celery, walnut and sage gremolata

This is a delicious dish for vegetarians – but it is also very good with the addition of 50 g (2 oz) of sautéed bacon.

75 g (3 oz) butter
225 g (8 oz) celery, thinly sliced
1 teaspoon sugar
4 tablespoons red wine
1 tablespoon balsamic vinegar
2 tablespoons olive oil
450 g (1 lb) penne pasta
salt and freshly ground pepper
freshly grated nutmeg

For the gremolata:
50 g (2 oz) walnuts
75 g (3 oz) fresh white breadcrumbs
½ garlic clove, crushed
1 tablespoon chopped fresh sage

Heat 25 g (1 oz) of the butter in a frying pan, add the celery and sugar and cook until soft and lightly golden. Pour in the wine and vinegar and continue cooking to form a lightly caramelized glaze around the celery.

Place all the ingredients for the gremolata in a liquidizer and blend together.

Heat the remaining butter in a frying pan with the olive oil, add the gremolata and cook until golden and crunchy.

Cook the pasta in boiling salted water until al dente (just tender, but still firm to the bite). Drain and mix with the caramelized celery. Taste and adjust the seasoning and serve hot, sprinkled with the gremolata.

Fettuccine with charred tomatoes and rosemary oil

If you know someone who owns a rosemary bush, you have a supply of fresh rosemary all year round. This hardy herb is not just for use with lamb. Here it makes a tasty oil for a simple pasta dish.

450 g (1 lb) small plum tomatoes, halved
1 garlic clove, lightly crushed
1 tablespoon sugar
salt and freshly ground pepper
450 g (1 lb) fettuccine pasta
6 tablespoons olive oil
40 g (1½ oz) fresh rosemary
freshly grated nutmeg

Preheat the oven to 200°C/400°F/Gas Mark 6.

Place the halved tomatoes on a lightly greased baking sheet, rub each with half of the garlic, then sprinkle with sugar and a little salt and pepper. Bake the tomatoes for 10–15 minutes or until soft and slightly charred. Alternatively, place them under a hot grill to achieve the same result.

Cook the pasta in boiling salted water until al dente (just tender, but still firm to the bite), then drain.

Place the olive oil, rosemary and remaining garlic in a liquidizer and blend to a purée. Season to taste. Toss the pasta with the rosemary oil and adjust the seasoning with salt, pepper and nutmeg. Top with the charred tomatoes and serve at once.

Rigatoni with white bean hummus

450 g (1 lb) rigatoni pasta
6 tablespoons olive oil
4 tablespoons chopped fresh parsley
150 ml (¼ pint) White Bean Hummus (page 39)
salt and freshly ground black pepper

Cook the pasta in boiling salted water until al dente
(just tender, but still firm to the bite). Drain the
pasta, retaining a little of the cooking water.

Return the pasta to the pan, add the olive oil
and parsley, then carefully stir in the white bean
hummus and a little of the cooking water to form
a sauce around the pasta. Season with salt and a
good sprinkling of freshly ground black pepper and
serve hot.

Parsley mash gnocchi with blue cheese

900 g (2 lb) potatoes (Cara or Maris Piper), peeled
salt and freshly ground pepper
275 g (10 oz) plain flour
1 egg
freshly grated nutmeg
25 g (1 oz) fresh parsley, chopped

For the blue cheese sauce:
150 g (5 oz) cold butter, cut into small pieces
100 g (4 oz) blue cheese (e.g. Stilton), crumbled

Place the potatoes in a saucepan, cover with water,
add a good pinch of salt and bring to the boil. Cook
until tender, drain well and then dry in a clean tea
towel. Rub the potatoes through a fine sieve into a
large bowl. Add the flour, egg, salt, pepper and nutmeg to taste. Mix well together, add the parsley and
beat to form a smooth dough.

With floured hands, roll the dough into long,
2 cm (¾ inch) diameter cylinders, then cut into 2 cm
(¾ inch) pieces. Using a fork, make an indentation
on each piece. Place the gnocchi on a floured tray
until ready to cook.

Bring a large saucepan of salted water to the boil,
then reduce to a simmer, add the gnocchi and poach
gently for 3–4 minutes or until they rise to the surface of the water. Drain them well and keep warm in
a buttered serving dish.

To make the sauce, boil 125 ml (4 fl oz) water in
a small saucepan, whisk in the pieces of cold butter
a few at a time, then whisk in the blue cheese and
season to taste. Toss the gnocchi with the sauce and
serve at once.

Trenette with tuna and tomatoes

6 tablespoons olive oil
225 g (8 oz) flat mushrooms, cut into small dice
1 tablespoon dried oregano
1 tablespoon chopped fresh parsley
400 g (14 oz) canned tomatoes, drained and roughly chopped
2 tablespoons tomato purée
sugar
200 g (7 oz) canned tuna, drained and flaked
salt and freshly ground pepper
450 g (1 lb) trenette pasta or spaghettini
freshly grated nutmeg

Heat half the olive oil in a frying pan, add the diced
mushrooms and cook over a fairly high heat until
lightly golden. Add the oregano and half the parsley.

Add the roughly chopped tomatoes, the tomato
purée and a pinch of sugar and cook over a low heat
until the sauce thickens. Add the flaked tuna and
gently stir into the sauce. Season to taste and stir in
the remaining oil. Keep warm.

Cook the pasta in boiling salted water until al
dente (just tender, but still firm to the bite). Drain
well, return to the pan and season with salt, pepper
and nutmeg. Place the pasta in a serving dish and
pour over the tuna sauce. Sprinkle with the remaining
chopped parsley and serve at once.

Penne with spring vegetables and mint

2 rashers of streaky bacon, cut into small pieces
100 g (4 oz) frozen (or fresh) peas
100 g (4 oz) frozen (or fresh) broad beans, blanched
  and skinned
100 g (4 oz) young leeks, cut into 5 mm (¼ inch) slices
450 ml (¾ pint) chicken stock
4 tablespoons olive oil
50 g (2 oz) butter
450 g (1 lb) penne pasta
2 tablespoons shredded fresh mint leaves

Heat a heavy-bottomed saucepan, add the bacon and fry until the bacon releases its juices and becomes crisp. Remove from the pan and set aside.

Add the peas, beans and leeks to the pan, cover with the stock and cook until the vegetables are tender. Lift out the vegetables with a slotted spoon and keep warm.

Boil the stock over a high heat until reduced to about 150 ml (¼ pint), then whisk in the oil and butter.

Meanwhile, cook the pasta in boiling water until al dente (just tender, but still firm to the bite). Drain well, then add to the sauce and return the vegetables to the pan, add the mint, toss well together and serve at once, sprinkled with the crisp bacon.

Spaghetti with potatoes and wilted beans

This dish originates from Liguria in Italy. I love the peasanty feel to it – as well as the fact that it's all cooked in one pan and there isn't too much washing up to do!

3 waxy potatoes, cut into 1 cm (½ inch) cubes
150 g (5 oz) trimmed green beans
450 g (1 lb) spaghetti
1 small jar of pesto sauce, about 125 ml (4 fl oz)
2 tablespoons grated Parmesan cheese (optional)

Boil the potatoes in a large saucepan of lightly salted water until tender but still retaining their shape. Using a slotted spoon, transfer the potatoes from the water to a bowl. Add the beans to the same water and boil until fairly well cooked and soft, then remove and add to the potatoes.

Now add the spaghetti to the pan and cook until al dente (just tender, but still firm to the bite). Drain the spaghetti well, retaining 125 ml (4 fl oz) of the cooking liquid.

Mix the reserved cooking liquid with the pesto sauce. Add the spaghetti to the potatoes and beans, together with the sauce, and toss to combine. Taste and adjust the seasoning if required. Serve at once, with grated Parmesan if liked.

Spaghetti with chicken liver sauce

Sprinkle with chopped fresh basil and Parmesan for a real treat!

6 tablespoons vegetable oil
½ onion, finely chopped
1 carrot, finely chopped
400 g (14 oz) canned tomatoes, drained and finely chopped
pinch of sugar
125 ml (4 fl oz) red wine
175 g (6 oz) fresh chicken livers, cut into small pieces
salt and freshly ground pepper
pinch of paprika
1 large garlic clove, crushed
75 g (3 oz) black pudding, sliced
450 g (1 lb) spaghetti

Heat half the oil in a saucepan, add the onion and carrot and cook until tender. Add the tomatoes and sugar and cook for 10 minutes, until the tomatoes become thick and sauce-like. Pour in the red wine and simmer for a further 2 minutes, then remove from the heat and keep warm.

Heat the remaining oil in a frying pan. Season the livers with salt, pepper and paprika and toss in the garlic. Sauté the livers over a high heat until firm and brown on the outside, but retaining their pink interior. Add the sliced black pudding, toss together for a further minute, then add the tomato sauce.

Cook the pasta in boiling water until just tender, but still firm to the bite. Drain well, season and place in a serving dish. Coat with the chicken liver sauce and serve at once.

Hot dog fusilli

This dish evolved from the original £1 challenge.
Frankfurter sausages are sold in cans or vacuum-
packed, or you could use standard pork sausages –
it's a very versatile recipe.

6 tablespoons olive oil
225 g (8 oz) frankfurter sausages, blanched in boiling water
    for 3 minutes, chilled and sliced 1 cm (½ inch) thick
1 teaspoon dried sage or mixed herbs
½ garlic clove, crushed
pinch of dried chilli flakes
200 g (7 oz) canned tomatoes, with juice, chopped
salt and freshly ground pepper
450 g (1 lb) fusilli pasta
4 tablespoons grated Parmesan cheese (optional)

Heat 2 tablespoons of the oil in a frying pan, add
the sliced sausage and cook until golden. Stir in the
herbs, then remove the sausages from the pan and
keep warm.

Add a little more oil to the pan, then add the garlic,
chilli and tomatoes and cook until the tomatoes have
thickened slightly and become separated from the
oil. Season to taste and keep warm.

Cook the fusilli in plenty of boiling salted water
until al dente (just tender, but still firm to the bite),
then drain and return to the pan. Add the tomato
sauce and the sausages and toss together. Heat
through gently, taste and adjust the seasoning and
serve hot.

Open pasta with scrambled eggs and mussels

The idea of pasta with mussels, mint and scrambled egg may sound strange, but try it and you will be surprised how well they work together.

450 g (1 lb) mussels, scrubbed
5 tablespoons dry white wine
4 tablespoons double cream
8 lasagne sheets, fresh or dried
4 eggs, beaten
salt and freshly ground pepper
50 g (2 oz) butter
1 tablespoon fresh mint, chopped

Place the mussels in a saucepan, add the wine and 150 ml (¼ pint) water. Bring to the boil, cover with a lid and cook over a high heat for 2 minutes or until the shells open. Drain the mussels in a colander, reserving the cooking liquid. Leave to cool slightly, then remove the mussels from their shells and remove their beards.

Strain the mussel cooking liquid into a clean pan and boil over a high heat to reduce it to half its original volume. Add the cream and reduce again until the sauce thickens enough to coat the back of a spoon. Strain through a fine sieve and keep warm.

Cook the lasagne in boiling salted water until al dente (just tender, but still firm to the bite), then drain.

Break the eggs into a bowl and whisk them together with a little salt and pepper. Heat the butter in a saucepan, pour in the eggs and cook, stirring, until creamy.

To serve, add the mussels and mint to the sauce. Lay a sheet of pasta on each plate, top with the scrambled egg and coat with the mussel sauce, then top with another pasta sheet. Serve at once.

Linguine with garlic-chilli oil

125ml (4 fl oz) olive oil
salt and freshly ground pepper
450 g (1 lb) linguine pasta
3 garlic cloves, crushed
½ teaspoon dried chilli flakes
1 tablespoon chopped fresh parsley
freshly grated nutmeg

Bring a large saucepan of water to the boil with 2 tablespoons of the oil and a little salt. Add the pasta and cook until al dente (just tender, but still firm to the bite).

Meanwhile, prepare the sauce. Heat the remaining olive oil in a saucepan, add the garlic and chilli flakes and cook over a low heat for 1–2 minutes.

When the pasta is cooked, drain it in a colander, then add it to the garlic and chilli oil, toss together gently, add the parsley and season to taste with salt, pepper and nutmeg. Serve hot.

Peking style meatballs with noodles

450 g (1 lb) belly pork, minced
4 teaspoons dry sherry
8 tablespoons dark soy sauce
2 garlic cloves, crushed
1/4 teaspoon ground ginger
4 spring onions, finely shredded
salt and freshly ground pepper
sugar
1 egg yolk
2 tablespoons cornflour
300 g (11 oz) oriental egg noodles (or similar pasta)
4 tablespoons vegetable oil

Place the minced pork in a bowl, add the sherry and half the soy sauce, the garlic, ginger, spring onions, salt, pepper and a pinch of sugar. Add the egg yolk and mix well, then stir in the cornflour. Leave the mixture in the refrigerator to rest for 30 minutes.

Cook the noodles as directed on the packet, then drain well.

Heat the vegetable oil in a frying pan. Shape the meat mixture into 2.5 cm (1 inch) balls and fry them until golden. Drain the meatballs and mix with the cooked noodles. Add the remaining soy sauce, mix in gently, then serve immediately.

Chicken liver risotto

100 g (4 oz) butter
½ onion, finely chopped
¼ teaspoon dried thyme
225 g (8 oz) arborio rice
3 tablespoons dry white wine
900 ml (1½ pints) chicken stock, hot
3 tablespoons vegetable oil
400 g (14 oz) chicken livers, cleaned and halved
6 tablespoons dry madeira, dry sherry or port
150 ml (¼ pint) double cream, lightly whipped

Melt 75 g (3 oz) of the butter in a heavy-bottomed
frying pan, add the onion and thyme and cook over
a low heat until softened but not browned. Add the
rice and stir well to coat with the butter. Cook over
a low heat for 2 minutes until the rice becomes opaque.

Increase the heat, pour in the wine and cook for
4–5 minutes or until the wine has evaporated.

Add the stock a little at a time, stirring constantly,
adding more as it is absorbed, until about 600 ml
(1 pint) of stock has been used and the rice is tender
but retains a little bite (about 20–25 minutes).

Heat the oil and the remaining butter in a frying
pan, add the chicken livers and cook over a high
heat to seal in their juices. Remove from the pan
and keep warm. Add the madeira and the remaining
300 ml (½ pint) chicken stock to the pan and boil
to reduce to a syrupy consistency.

To finish the risotto, beat in the cream and a
little more butter, taste and adjust the seasoning if
required. Divide the risotto between four serving
dishes, top with the chicken livers and their sauce
and serve at once.

Crushed sweetcorn risotto with courgettes

100 g (4 oz) butter
½ onion, finely chopped
225 g (8 oz) arborio rice
600 ml (1 pint) chicken stock, hot
150 g (5 oz) frozen or canned sweetcorn
4 tablespoons single cream
75 g (3 oz) courgettes, sliced lengthways into ribbons
2 tablespoons chopped fresh mint
salt and freshly ground pepper

Melt 75 g (3 oz) of the butter in a heavy-bottomed frying pan, add the onion and cook over a low heat until tender. Add the rice and stir well to coat with the butter. Add a little of the stock and stir until the liquid has been absorbed.

Keep adding the stock a little at a time, stirring constantly, until the rice is tender but retains a little bite (about 20–25 minutes). Towards the end of the cooking time, add the stock in smaller quantities and check whether the rice is done. The final consistency should be loose but not sloppy.

Meanwhile, place the sweetcorn and cream in a liquidizer and blend to a coarse purée. Heat the remaining butter in a frying pan, add the courgettes and sauté until tender.

Add the sweetcorn purée to the risotto. Sprinkle the courgettes with the mint and a little salt and pepper and gently stir them into the risotto. Serve at once.

MAIN
COURSES

Bourride of smoked haddock

50 g (2 oz) butter
½ onion, chopped
1 garlic clove, crushed
100 g (4 oz) leeks, shredded
1 carrot, cut into 5 mm (¼ inch) dice
275 g (10 oz) potatoes, cut into 5 mm (¼ inch) dice
450 ml (¾ pint) fish stock
450 g (1 lb) smoked haddock
6 tablespoons mayonnaise

Heat the butter in a saucepan, add the onion, garlic and leeks and cook over a low heat for 5–8 minutes or until the vegetables are tender. Add the carrot and potato dice and cook for a further 5 minutes. Pour in the stock and bring to the boil, then reduce the heat and simmer for 10 minutes.

Add the smoked haddock and cook for 5 minutes. Using a slotted spoon, remove the haddock and vegetables and keep warm. Flake the fish into fairly large pieces.

Boil the stock over a high heat to reduce it to 250 ml (8 fl oz). Remove from the heat and beat in the mayonnaise. Return to the heat and bring to just below boiling point. Return the flaked fish and vegetables to the sauce and serve hot.

Kedgeree in filo purses

75 g (3 oz) butter
1/2 onion, chopped
2 teaspoons curry paste
225 g (8 oz) cooked rice (preferably basmati)
250 g (9 oz) smoked haddock, cooked and flaked
3 eggs, hard-boiled and chopped
5 tablespoons double cream
salt and freshly ground black pepper
1 tablespoon chopped fresh coriander
8 sheets of filo pastry, 20 cm (8 inches) square

Heat half the butter in a large saucepan, add the onion and cook over a low heat until tender. Add the curry paste and stir to combine with the onion. Add the rice and mix well, then add the haddock and eggs and stir in gently so that you do not break up the fish. Add the cream, season to taste and transfer to a bowl. When cool, add the coriander and leave in the refrigerator for up to 1 hour.

Preheat the oven to 190°C/375°F/Gas Mark 5.

Melt the remaining butter. Place 4 filo pastry squares on a work surface and brush with a little of the butter. Set another square of filo on top of each one and spoon a quarter of the kedgeree mixture into the centre. Brush the edges of the pastry with a little more butter, then bring the sides up over the filling and pinch together to form purse shapes. Brush the outsides with butter, then bake for 12–15 minutes or until golden. Leave to cool slightly before serving.

Baked plaice with sardine tapenade

Canned sardines can be used if fresh are not available, but the result is not as good.

4 fresh plaice fillets, about 150 g (5 oz) each
salt and freshly ground pepper
8 small fresh sardine fillets, boneless, finely chopped
1 onion, finely chopped
2 tablespoons pitted black olives, finely chopped
1 tablespoon capers, drained and finely chopped
2 tablespoons fresh white breadcrumbs
6 tablespoons olive oil
1 tablespoon maple syrup
1 tablespoon white wine vinegar
3 tablespoons mustard
1 tablespoon chopped fresh chives

Preheat the oven to 190°C/375°F/Gas Mark 5.

Season the plaice fillets with a little salt and pepper. In a bowl, combine the sardines, onion, olives, capers and breadcrumbs. Add salt and pepper with care: you should not need much salt.

Spread the mixture on the plaice fillets, roll up and secure each fillet with a cocktail stick. Place on a baking sheet, spoon a little olive oil over each fillet and bake for 8–10 minutes.

Meanwhile, heat the maple syrup and vinegar together in a small saucepan, then whisk in the olive oil, mustard and chives.

Transfer the cooked plaice fillets to a serving dish and coat with the sauce; serve at once.

Grey mullet in 'acqua pazza'

This dish of mullet in 'crazy water' (acqua pazza) is simplicity itself; I learnt it when we hosted a culinary promotion with the hotel San Pietro from Positano in Italy.

4 fresh grey mullet fillets
2 garlic cloves, thinly sliced
5 tablespoons olive oil
¼ teaspoon dried chilli flakes
400 g (14 oz) canned plum tomatoes, drained and chopped
2 tablespoons chopped fresh parsley
1 teaspoon fresh or dried oregano
1 teaspoon anchovy essence (optional)
salt and freshly ground pepper

Remove all the bones from the grey mullet fillets and set aside.

Place 750 ml (1¼ pints) water in a wide saucepan or deep frying pan and bring to the boil. Add the garlic, olive oil and chilli flakes, reduce the heat and simmer for 10 minutes. Add the tomatoes, herbs and anchovy essence and simmer for a further 25 minutes; the mixture will reduce and thicken.

Season the fish with salt and pepper and add to the pan. Simmer for 10 minutes or until cooked. Serve with steamed potatoes drizzled with olive oil.

Baked cod with tomato and mustard sauce

This simple dish is elevated to gourmet status by serving it on a bed of creamy mashed potato to which you have added a generous spoonful of pesto sauce and a knob of butter. Sautéed courgettes are the ideal accompaniment.

4 fresh cod fillets, about 150 g (5 oz) each, boneless, cleaned
25 g (1 oz) butter
1 onion, finely chopped
1 tablespoon fennel seeds
pinch of mixed herbs
450 g (1 lb) fresh tomatoes, skinned, deseeded and roughly chopped
2 teaspoons English mustard
2 teaspoons brown sugar
salt and freshly ground pepper
pinch of cayenne pepper
1 tablespoon fresh chopped parsley

Preheat the oven to 190°C/375°F/Gas Mark 5. Place the fish in a lightly buttered ovenproof dish.

Heat the butter in a saucepan, add the onion and fry until tender. Add the fennel seeds, herbs, tomatoes, mustard and brown sugar. Mix well, then season to taste with salt, pepper and cayenne.

Pour the sauce over the fish and bake for 20–25 minutes. Sprinkle with fresh parsley and serve hot.

Shanghai fishburgers with cumin and ginger ketchup

450 g (1 lb) whiting or other white fish fillet
1 tablespoon finely chopped fresh root ginger
3 spring onions, finely chopped
1 tablespoon chopped fresh coriander
$1/4$ teaspoon dried chilli flakes
1 tablespoon soy sauce
2 eggs, beaten
1 tablespoon cornflour
salt and freshly ground pepper
4 tablespoons vegetable oil
2 baps
lettuce leaves, to serve

For the cumin and ginger ketchup:
6 tablespoons mayonnaise
1 tablespoon tomato ketchup
$1/4$ teaspoon ground cumin
$1/4$ teaspoon chopped fresh root ginger

Run your fingers over the fish and remove any small bones with tweezers. Mince the fish in a food processor and place in a bowl. Add the ginger, spring onions, coriander, chilli flakes and soy sauce and stir to mix. Bind the mixture with the eggs and cornflour, season lightly, then leave in the refrigerator for 1 hour.

Mix together all the ingredients for the ketchup in a small bowl.

Shape the chilled fish mixture into eight small burgers. Heat the oil in a frying pan and fry the fishburgers gently until golden, about 3–4 minutes on each side. Drain on paper towels.

Meanwhile, slice the baps in half and toast them, top with the lettuce and the hot fishburgers and serve at once, accompanied by the ketchup, and crisp, thin French fries.

Fresh salt cod on herb-braised potatoes

4 cod fillets, about 150 g (5 oz) each
1 tablespoon salt (preferably sea salt)
75 g (3 oz) butter
1 onion, thinly sliced
freshly ground pepper
450 g (1 lb) large potatoes
50 g (2 oz) selection of fresh herbs (thyme, rosemary,
   parsley), chopped
300 ml (½ pint) chicken stock, boiling
6 tablespoons olive oil

Place the fish fillets in a shallow dish, sprinkle evenly
with the salt and leave overnight in the refrigerator.

The next day, use 25 g (1 oz) of the butter to
grease an ovenproof serving dish. Preheat the oven
to 190°C/375°F/Gas Mark 5.

Heat 25 g (1 oz) of the butter in a frying pan and
fry the onion over a low heat until golden. Season
with salt and pepper.

Thinly slice the potatoes and layer them over the
base of the buttered dish, season and top with half
of the onion; add another layer of potato slices,
salt and pepper, the remaining onion and a final
layer of potatoes. Sprinkle on the herbs. Dot the top
layer of potatoes with the remaining butter, season
with salt and pepper and pour on the boiling stock.
Bake for 50 minutes or until tender and golden.

Heat the olive oil in a frying pan. Carefully wash
and dry the cod fillets, then fry them in the oil for
1 minute on each side or until golden.

Place the cod fillets on top of the potatoes, season
lightly with salt and pepper and return to the oven
for a further 8–10 minutes. Serve hot.

Cod tagine

4 cod (or other white fish) fillets, about 150 g (5 oz) each
8 tablespoons vegetable oil
2 tablespoons ground cumin
2 teaspoons turmeric
1 onion, chopped
1 garlic clove, crushed
2 potatoes, cut into 1 cm (½ inch) dice
2 carrots, cut into 1 cm (½ inch) dice
100 g (4 oz) pumpkin, cut into 1 cm (½ inch) dice
1 teaspoon ground ginger
1 teaspoon ground cinnamon
400 g (14 oz) canned cannellini beans
50 g (2 oz) prunes, soaked overnight and stoned
salt and freshly ground pepper

Place the cod in a shallow dish with 4 tablespoons
of the oil, the cumin and turmeric and leave to
marinate in the refrigerator for 1 hour.

Preheat the oven to 200°C/400°F/Gas Mark 6.

Heat the remaining oil in a large saucepan, add
the onion and garlic and cook over a low heat until
tender. Add the potatoes, carrots and pumpkin and
fry until golden, then add the ginger and cinnamon.
Reduce the heat and cook gently for 5 minutes.

Add the cannellini beans, prunes and 125 ml
(4 fl oz) water and cook until the vegetables are
tender. Taste and adjust the seasoning.

Place the fish on a baking sheet, brush with the
marinade and bake in the hot oven for 5–8 minutes
or until cooked. Serve the fish on a warmed plate,
surrounded by the tagine of vegetables and
accompanied by couscous.

Grilled mackerel with sweet and sour rhubarb

Mackerel is classically served with a gooseberry sauce; the point is that it needs a sharp flavour to offset the oiliness of the fish, such as this tangy rhubarb sauce.

4 tablespoons olive oil
200 g (7 oz) canned tomatoes, drained and finely chopped
325 g (12 oz) fresh rhubarb, peeled and cut into small
    chunks
3 tablespoons brown sugar
2 tablespoons balsamic vinegar
salt and freshly ground pepper
pinch of ground cinnamon
pinch of ground ginger
1 tablespoon chopped fresh coriander
4 fresh mackerel, about 400 g (14 oz) each

Heat half the olive oil in a wide saucepan, add the tomatoes and simmer over a low heat until they become thick and pulpy. Add the rhubarb, brown sugar and vinegar and bring to the boil, then reduce the heat and cook gently for 8–10 minutes or until the sauce is thick. Season to taste with salt, pepper, cinnamon and ginger; you may need to add a little more sugar if the rhubarb is very acidic. Add the fresh coriander to the sauce and keep warm.

Clean the mackerel, remove the fillets and cut three small incisions into the flesh on both sides. Season and brush them with the remaining olive oil. Place under a hot grill and cook for 5–6 minutes on each side or until golden and crisp.

Serve the grilled mackerel with the rhubarb sauce, accompanied by some sautéed aubergine slices.

Chargrilled mackerel with spicy tomato chutney

4 tablespoons olive oil
1 garlic clove, crushed
juice of ½ lemon
¼ teaspoon ground cumin
4 fresh mackerel fillets
salt and freshly ground pepper

For the chutney:
600 ml (1 pint) red wine vinegar
75 g (3 oz) sugar
small pinch of cayenne pepper
pinch of ground cinnamon
½ teaspoon dried chilli flakes
400 g (14 oz) canned peeled tomatoes, chopped
1 apple (preferably Granny Smith), peeled and chopped
½ onion, chopped

First make the chutney. Place the vinegar, sugar, cayenne, cinnamon and chilli flakes in a saucepan and bring to the boil, stirring until the sugar dissolves. Lower the heat, add the tomatoes, apple and onion and simmer gently for 25–30 minutes or until thick. Leave to cool.

Meanwhile, mix the oil, garlic, lemon juice and cumin in a shallow dish. Season the fish fillets and add to the marinade; leave for 30 minutes.

Grill the fish on a barbecue or under a hot grill until crisp. Serve with the tomato chutney and a small green salad.

Salmon cakes with anchovy aïoli

400 g (14 oz) fresh salmon fillet
225 g (8 oz) fresh white breadcrumbs
125 ml (4 fl oz) milk
salt and freshly ground black pepper
100 g (4 oz) flour
2 eggs, beaten
4 tablespoons vegetable oil

For the anchovy aïoli:
100 g (4 oz) mayonnaise
1 garlic clove, crushed
2 teaspoons anchovy essence

Run your fingers over the fish and remove any small bones with tweezers. Mince the salmon finely in a food processor.

Place half the breadcrumbs in a bowl with the milk and leave for 5 minutes, then squeeze out all the moisture. Add the salmon to the soaked breadcrumbs, season with salt and pepper and mix together well. Shape the mixture into ovals about 2 cm (3/4 inch) thick.

Mix the ingredients for the anchovy aïoli in a small bowl.

Season the flour with salt and pepper. Put the seasoned flour, the beaten eggs and the remaining breadcrumbs in three shallow dishes. Coat the salmon cakes first in flour, then in egg, then in breadcrumbs.

Heat the oil in a frying pan, add the salmon cakes and fry for 4–5 minutes on each side, until cooked and golden.

Drain on paper towels and serve hot, with the anchovy aïoli.

Braised chicken with anchovies and olives

8 chicken thighs
8 chicken drumsticks
salt and freshly ground pepper
3 tablespoons olive oil
2 garlic cloves, crushed
150 ml (5 fl oz) dry white wine
2 tablespoons balsamic vinegar
600 ml (1 pint) chicken stock
75 g (3 oz) pitted black olives
4 anchovy fillets, rinsed to remove excess salt, drained
    and chopped

Cut three incisions in each of the chicken pieces and
season lightly. Heat the oil in a flameproof casserole,
add the seasoned chicken pieces and cook until
golden brown all over.

Add the garlic and stir to mix, then pour in the
wine and the vinegar and bring to the boil. Add the
stock, olives and anchovies. Cover with a lid and
simmer gently for 40–45 minutes or until the chicken
is cooked and tender. Serve with buttery noodles.

Grilled chicken wings on drunken black beans with chilli verde

Instead of the chicken wings, I also like to make this dish with lambs' kidneys or pork chops.

175 g (6 oz) black turtle beans, picked over and rinsed
1 garlic clove, crushed
1 tablespoon ground cumin
100 ml (3½ fl oz) lager
3 tablespoons olive oil
salt and freshly ground pepper
8 chicken wings

For the chilli verde:
½ green pepper, deseeded
1 green chilli, deseeded
3 tablespoons chopped fresh coriander
3 spring onions, finely chopped
2 tablespoons white wine vinegar
½ teaspoon mustard
3 tablespoons olive oil

To make the chilli verde, place the pepper, chilli, coriander and spring onions in a liquidizer and blend to a coarse purée. Transfer to a mixing bowl, add the vinegar, mustard and oil. Season to taste. Leave at room temperature to allow the flavours to infuse.

Place the black beans in a saucepan, cover with cold water, add the garlic and cumin and bring to the boil. Reduce the heat and simmer gently for about 1 hour or until tender. Add the beer towards the end of the cooking time. When the beans are cooked, the liquid will have reduced and formed a sauce around them. Add the olive oil and season to taste.

Grill the chicken wings under a hot grill or over a barbecue. Arrange the wings on the black beans, drizzle over the chilli verde and serve hot.

Barbecue spice rub chicken

8 chicken thighs
8 chicken drumsticks

For the spice rub:
½ teaspoon salt
½ teaspoon sugar
½ teaspoon brown sugar
½ teaspoon dried chilli flakes
½ teaspoon black pepper
½ teaspoon paprika
¼ teaspoon ground cumin
¼ teaspoon cayenne pepper

Combine all the ingredients for the spice rub in a large bowl. Using a sharp knife, cut three incisions in each of the chicken pieces to allow the spices to permeate the flesh. Add the chicken to the dry ingredients and leave for 2 hours.

Cook on a barbecue or under a hot grill. Serve with a yoghurt and fresh herb dressing and a leafy mixed salad.

Palak chicken

Palak is Gujarati for spinach. This is a rich-tasting spicy chicken dish that's deceptively simple to make.

6 tablespoons vegetable oil
12 chicken wings
1 onion, finely chopped
1 garlic clove, crushed
1 tablespoon ground ginger
1/2 teaspoon dried chilli flakes
1/4 teaspoon turmeric (optional)
1 teaspoon ground cumin
1 teaspoon ground coriander
200 g (7 oz) fresh spinach, chopped,
   or frozen puréed spinach
200 g (7 oz) canned plum tomatoes, chopped
300 ml (1/2 pint) chicken stock
2 tablespoons yoghurt

Heat 2 tablespoons of the oil in a frying pan until very hot, add the chicken wings and fry until golden. Remove the chicken from the pan and drain.

Add the onion and garlic to the pan and fry until lightly browned. Add the spices and cook for 3–5 minutes.

Return the chicken to the pan, add the spinach, then add the tomatoes, stock and remaining oil. Bring to the boil, reduce the heat and simmer until tender, about 20 minutes (it may be necessary to add a little water during cooking).

Add the yogurt and stir into the sauce. Serve hot, with basmati rice.

Chicken and mustard pot pie

50 g (2 oz) butter
8 chicken legs, cut into 2 pieces
salt and freshly ground black pepper
50 g (2 oz) flour
900 ml (1½ pints) chicken stock
100 g (4 oz) button mushrooms, cut in half
1 tablespoon mild English mustard
250 g (9 oz) prepared puff pastry
1 egg, beaten

Gently heat the butter in a frying pan, add the seasoned chicken pieces and fry until sealed, but do not let the chicken brown. Sprinkle the flour over the chicken and cook for 2–3 minutes.

Gradually stir in the stock, mixing well to form a light sauce around the chicken. Bring to the boil, then reduce the heat, cover and simmer until just tender. Add the mushrooms and cook for a further 5 minutes. Stir in the mustard and season to taste. Leave to cool.

Preheat the oven to 190°C/375°F/Gas Mark 5. Transfer the chicken mixture to a pie dish.

Roll out the pastry and cover the pie. Brush the pastry with beaten egg to glaze. Bake for 25 minutes, until the pastry is puffed and golden. Serve hot, with your favourite vegetables.

Bstila of chicken with sweet spices

75 g (3 oz) butter
2 large chicken breasts
225 g (8 oz) fresh chicken livers
salt and freshly ground pepper
1 small onion, chopped
½ teaspoon crushed garlic
¼ teaspoon turmeric
¼ teaspoon ground ginger
¼ teaspoon ground cumin
¼ teaspoon ground allspice
a little chicken stock (optional)
1 egg
75 g (3 oz) almonds, toasted
1 teaspoon ground cinnamon, plus extra for dusting
½ teaspoon sugar
100 g (4 oz) cooked rice (preferably basmati)
2 tablespoons chopped fresh coriander or parsley
pinch of cayenne pepper
4 sheets of filo pastry, about 20 cm (8 inches) square
a little egg wash

Preheat the oven to 180°C/350°F/Gas Mark 4.

Heat the butter in a frying pan and fry the lightly seasoned chicken breasts and livers over a high heat until golden. Remove from the pan. Add the onion and garlic to the pan with the turmeric, ginger, cumin and allspice and cook for 1 minute to release their fragrance. Return the chicken breasts to the pan, half cover with stock or water and bring to the boil. Reduce the heat and simmer for 8 minutes. Add the livers and cook for a further 2–3 minutes. Remove the breasts and livers from the pan and cut them into 2 cm (¾ inch) dice.

Boil the cooking liquid until it becomes syrupy in consistency. Leave to cool slightly, then whisk in the egg.

In a bowl, mix together the almonds, cinnamon, sugar and cooked rice. Add the fresh herbs and cayenne pepper.

Place two sheets of filo pastry in a baking tin about 20 cm (8 inches) square. Brush with the sauce and egg mixture, then add the diced chicken and livers. Top with the rice mixture, add the remaining sauce, then cover with the remaining filo pastry and tuck down the sides. Brush with egg wash and a light criss-cross dusting of cinnamon. Bake for 15–20 minutes or until golden. Serve hot.

Turkey osso buco

1 large turkey leg, sawn through the bone into 5 cm
   (2 inch) 'steaks'
3–4 tablespoons flour
salt and freshly ground pepper
3 tablespoons vegetable oil
25 g (1 oz) butter
1 onion, finely chopped
2 carrots, cut into very small dice
2 sticks of celery, cut into very small dice
½ leek, cut into very small dice
1 garlic clove, crushed
1 tablespoon tomato purée
4 tablespoons dry white wine
2 tablespoons fresh orange juice
600 ml (1 pint) chicken stock

Preheat the oven to 160°C/325°F/Gas Mark 3.

Remove the sinews and any small bones from the turkey steaks. Coat the turkey with flour, seasoned with salt and pepper. Heat the oil in a saucepan or flameproof casserole wide enough to take the turkey steaks in one layer. Brown the turkey on both sides in the hot oil, then remove and set aside. Drain off any excess oil and add the butter to the pan.

Add the onion, carrots, celery, leek and garlic and cook over a low heat until the vegetables are tender. Add the tomato purée and stir in. Cook over a low heat for 2–3 minutes.

Add the wine and orange juice and boil for 3–4 minutes. Pour in the stock and return to the boil, adding a little salt and pepper.

Return the turkey to the pan, cover with a lid and place in the oven for 1–1½ hours. Alternatively, simmer on top of the cooker. Serve hot, with seasonal vegetables and, if you like, risotto, which is the classic accompaniment to osso buco.

Daube of rabbit with orange, cinnamon and rosemary

4 large fresh rabbit legs
salt and freshly ground pepper
½ tablespoon ground cinnamon
3-4 tablespoons flour
3 tablespoons olive oil
25 g (1 oz) butter
1 onion, finely chopped
1 garlic clove, crushed
1 tablespoon roughly chopped fresh rosemary
150 ml (5 fl oz) red wine
600 ml (1 pint) chicken stock
200 g (7 oz) canned tomatoes, chopped
50 ml (2 fl oz) orange juice
sugar

Preheat the oven to 180°C/350°F/Gas Mark 4.

Season the rabbit legs with salt, pepper and cinnamon. Dust them in the flour. Heat the oil in a flameproof casserole, add the rabbit legs and fry until golden and sealed. Remove from the pan and set aside.

Drain off any excess fat, add the butter and the onion and cook over a low heat until tender. Add the garlic and rosemary and cook for a further 1 minute. Pour in the red wine and bring to the boil, then add the stock and reduce the heat.

Return the legs to the sauce, add the chopped tomatoes, orange juice, a good pinch of sugar and a little salt and pepper. Cover with a lid and cook in the oven for 1 hour or until tender. Serve with polenta beaten with plenty of butter.

Spicy herb sausages in batter pudding

My version of an old British favourite, 'toad in the hole'.

450 g (1 lb) good-quality pork sausagemeat
1 tablespoon chopped fresh coriander
1 tablespoon fresh oregano leaves
1/4 teaspoon dried chilli flakes
1/4 teaspoon ground ginger
1 teaspoon mustard
4 spring onions, finely shredded
salt and freshly ground pepper
75 g (3 oz) plain flour
2 eggs
75 ml (3 fl oz) milk mixed with 50 ml (2 fl oz) water
3 tablespoons vegetable oil
2 tablespoons caraway seeds (optional)

Place the sausagemeat in a bowl and add the herbs, chilli, ginger, mustard and spring onions; mix in gently. Shape into eight small flat rounds and season with salt and pepper.

Sift the flour into a bowl, make a well in the centre, add the eggs and the milk and water and mix to form a paste. Beat until smooth, then strain and leave to stand for 30 minutes.

Preheat the oven to 200°C/400°F/Gas Mark 6. Grease one large baking tin or eight individual moulds with a little of the oil and place in the oven.

Heat the remaining oil in a frying pan and fry the sausage rounds for 1 minute on each side or until golden and sealed.

Pour the batter mix into the hot baking tin (or into the small moulds), add the sausage rounds and cook in the hot oven until risen and light in texture, about 30–35 minutes. If you like, sprinkle on the caraway seeds after about 20–25 minutes.

Chocolate chilli glazed pork

675 g (1½ lb) pork belly, cut into strips
salt and freshly ground pepper
4 fresh red chillies, deseeded
2 tablespoons clear honey, warmed
50 g (2 oz) bitter chocolate, melted

Preheat the oven to 200°C/400°F/Gas Mark 6.
Season the pork, then roast in the hot oven for
30–35 minutes or until golden.

Meanwhile, in a liquidizer, blend the chillies
and the honey; pour into a bowl, add the melted
chocolate and mix well.

Remove the pork from the oven, drain on paper
towels, brush with the chocolate glaze and return to
the oven for 10 minutes.

Serve on a bed of crisp mixed vegetables stir-fried
with a little chopped fresh ginger.

Braised blade of pork

If you can arrange your oven to take two casserole dishes, this satisfying dinner is even easier and more economical.

600 g (1¼ lb) blade of pork, boneless
6 dried prunes, soaked overnight and drained
salt and freshly ground pepper
2 tablespoons vegetable oil
300 ml (½ pint) red wine
1 litre (1¾ pints) chicken stock

For the red cabbage:
1 red cabbage, about 400 g (14 oz)
100 g (4 oz) butter
4 tablespoons white wine vinegar
15 g (½ oz) sugar
3 tablespoons redcurrant jelly

Preheat the oven to 200°C/400°F/Gas Mark 6. Take a knife or, better still, a kitchen steel and push a hole through the centre of the pork. Fill the hole with the soaked prunes, pushing them in with your fingers. Season the pork with salt and pepper.

Heat the oil in a flameproof casserole and fry the pork until golden and sealed on all sides.

Drain off the excess oil, then pour in the wine and bring to the boil for 2 minutes. Pour in the stock, cover with a tight-fitting lid and place in the hot oven for 1½ hours or until tender. During the cooking, baste the pork several times with the wine and stock.

Cut the cabbage into quarters, remove the central core and the faded outside leaves. Cut the cabbage into fine shreds. Heat the butter in a saucepan or flameproof casserole, add the cabbage, vinegar, sugar and 600 ml (1 pint) water. Bring to the boil, then cover with a lid and simmer for 45 minutes–1 hour or until the cabbage is tender. Alternatively, cook in the oven with the pork. When the cabbage is tender, remove the lid and boil to reduce any remaining liquid to a syrup. Add the redcurrant jelly to form a light glaze around the cabbage and season to taste.

To serve, slice the braised pork and serve on a bed of the red cabbage, with some of the braising juices poured over. A tart apple purée goes well with this dish.

Korean-style barbecue lamb ribs

900 g (2 lb) breast of lamb, cut into 10 cm (4 inch)
    lengths (ask your butcher)
salt and freshly ground pepper
4 tablespoons tomato ketchup
6 tablespoons soy sauce
½ tablespoon mustard
1 garlic clove, crushed
1 tablespoon sugar
1 tablespoon white wine vinegar
½ teaspoon ground ginger
3 teaspoons sesame seeds

Season the ribs with salt and pepper. Combine all
the remaining ingredients together and coat the ribs
in the mixture. Leave to marinate for up to 2 hours.

Place on a hot barbecue and grill for 20–25
minutes or until tender and slightly burnt on the
edges. Alternatively, cook in a hot oven at 200°C/
400°F/ Gas Mark 6. Serve hot.

Persian koftas with pitta toasts

400 g (14 oz) lean minced lamb
50 g (2 oz) cooked rice
1 onion, finely chopped or grated
1 teaspoon ground cinnamon
1 teaspoon ground cumin
salt and freshly ground pepper
2 eggs, beaten
3–4 tablespoons seasoned flour
75 g (3 oz) butter
1 tablespoon olive oil
4 pitta breads

For the salad:
75 g (3 oz) cucumber, cut into 1 cm (½ inch) dice
1 red onion, cut into 1 cm (½ inch) dice
½ garlic clove, crushed
4 tomatoes, deseeded and cut into 1 cm (½ inch) dice
4 tablespoons olive oil
juice of ½ lemon
2 tablespoons fresh coriander, chopped

Place the minced lamb in a bowl, add the rice, onion, spices, salt and pepper and mix well. Add one of the eggs to bind the mixture. Wetting your hands with water, shape the lamb mixture into oval balls. Place in the refrigerator until ready to cook.

For the salad, mix all the ingredients together; season to taste.

When ready to cook, soak eight or more bamboo skewers in cold water for 30 minutes. Preheat the grill or barbecue. Roll the meatballs in the seasoned flour, then in the remaining beaten egg. Thread them on to the skewers and grill, turning from time to time, until cooked and browned, about 15 minutes. Alternatively, heat the oil and butter in a frying pan and fry the meatballs until crisp and browned. Toast the pitta breads and fill with the koftas and salad.

Mexican lamb pasties

2 tablespoons vegetable oil
225 g (8 oz) minced lamb
1 onion, finely chopped
½ teaspoon dried chilli flakes
½ tablespoon fresh or dried thyme
½ tablespoon curry powder
1 tablespoon tomato purée
300 ml (½ pint) chicken stock or water
3 tablespoons fresh white breadcrumbs
salt and freshly ground pepper

For the pastry:
225 g (8 oz) flour
½ teaspoon salt
75 g (3 oz) cold margarine or butter, diced

First make the pastry: sift the flour and salt into a
bowl, add the butter or margarine and rub in with
your fingertips until the mixture resembles fine
breadcrumbs. Gradually add 4 tablespoons water to
make a dough. Wrap in greaseproof paper and leave
in the refrigerator to rest for up to 1 hour before use.

For the filling, heat the oil in a frying pan and fry
the lamb until well browned. Add the onion, chilli
flakes, thyme and curry powder, and cook for a
further 5 minutes. Stir in the tomato purée and the
chicken stock or water, reduce the heat and simmer
for 10 minutes, until the liquid thickens and forms
a sauce around the lamb. Fold in the breadcrumbs,
taste and adjust the seasoning and leave to cool.

Preheat the oven to 200°C/400°F/Gas Mark 6.
Divide the dough into eight equal balls and roll out
to circles about 15 cm (6 inches) in diameter.

Divide the meat into eight portions and spoon on to one half of each circle of dough. Fold the other half over to form half moons or turnovers; press the edges together and crimp with a fork.

Bake the pasties for 15–20 minutes or until golden, and serve straight from the oven.

Lamb short ribs with Tunisian spices

This dish is especially good served with couscous or tabouleh salad.

900 g (2 lb) breast of lamb, cut into 10 cm (4 inch) lengths
   (ask your butcher)
2 garlic cloves
1 tablespoon dried oregano
¼ teaspoon ground coriander
1 teaspoon ground cumin
6 tablespoons olive oil
good pinch of ground pepper
juice of 1 lemon
pinch of salt
2 tablespoons honey

Put the lamb ribs in a shallow, non-metallic dish. Mix all the remaining ingredients – except the honey – and pour over the ribs. Leave to marinate for at least 4 hours.

Remove the meat from the marinade and cook under a hot grill or on a barbecue, using the honey and the marinade to baste the lamb as it cooks. Serve when crisp and well browned.

VEGETARIAN
DISHES

Potato tortilla with rosemary and lemon

275 g (10 oz) new potatoes
salt and freshly ground pepper
1 garlic clove, halved
6 tablespoons olive oil
1 tablespoon chopped fresh rosemary
grated zest of ½ lemon
5 eggs
2 spring onions, shredded

Place the potatoes in a saucepan, cover with cold water, add salt and bring to the boil. Reduce the heat and cook until just tender. Drain and leave to cool.

When cold, cut the potatoes into thick slices. Rub a 20 cm (8 inch) omelette pan with the garlic clove. Heat 4 tablespoons of the oil, add the potato slices and cook over a low heat until golden. Add half the rosemary and the lemon zest and toss well to mix.

Beat the eggs in a bowl, season with salt and pepper and add the spring onions. Pour the mixture over the potatoes and cook over a fairly high heat for 1 minute or until the egg sets underneath. Carefully turn the omelette over and cook the other side. Sprinkle over the remaining rosemary and drizzle on the remaining oil; serve warm.

Bang bang potatoes

450 g (1 lb) potatoes, peeled
pinch of salt
4 tablespoons peanut butter
1 tablespoon vegetable oil
1 tablespoon chilli oil (or ½ tablespoon Tabasco sauce
    mixed with vegetable oil)
1 teaspoon sugar
2 tablespoons lemon juice
1 crisp head of lettuce, shredded, to serve

Cook the potatoes in boiling salted water, cool
and cut into 1 cm (½ inch) dice. Mix the peanut
butter, both oils, sugar and 6 tablespoons water in a
saucepan and gently bring to the boil. When it boils
you will find that the sauce thickens and becomes
smooth and shiny. Remove from the heat and leave
to cool.

Add the potatoes to the peanut sauce and mix
together gently so as not to break up the potatoes.
Season with salt and add the lemon juice.

Place on a bed of shredded lettuce and serve at
room temperature.

Muffin pizzas

A simple, convenient and delicious alternative to the pizza base, with some of my favourite toppings.

8 muffins, olive oil

Halve the muffins, brush with olive oil and toast them lightly under a hot grill, then add your choice of topping.

Garlic mushroom

200 g (7 oz) canned tomatoes, drained and chopped
2 tablespoons olive oil
1 garlic clove, crushed
100 g (4 oz) button mushrooms, sliced
1 tablespoon capers
fresh or dried oregano
salt and freshly ground pepper

Place the tomatoes in a small saucepan and cook over a high heat until they become quite thick and pulpy. Leave to cool.

Heat the oil in a frying pan, add the garlic and mushrooms and cook for 2 minutes. Add the capers and oregano, mix together and season to taste. Spread the toasted muffins with the tomato mixture, then top with the mushrooms. Place under a hot grill for 3–4 minutes.

Napoletana

8 fresh ripe tomatoes
2 tablespoons olive oil
1 onion, chopped
4–5 fresh sage leaves, chopped
50 g (2 oz) black olives, pitted and chopped
2 anchovy fillets, drained and chopped (optional for vegetarians!)
Cheddar cheese, grated

Cut the tomatoes into 5 mm (¼ inch) slices.

Heat the oil in a small frying pan and add the onion, sage, olives and anchovies, if using. Cook until the onion is tender.

Arrange the tomato slices on the toasted muffins, spoon on the olive mixture, then top with grated cheese. Place under a hot grill for 3–4 minutes or until golden and bubbling.

Blue cheese and walnut

4 tablespoons olive oil
1 red onion, thinly sliced
1/4 teaspoon dried sage
100 g (4 oz) blue cheese
   (e.g. Gorgonzola)
2 tablespoons milk
2 tablespoons walnuts,
   toasted and roughly
   chopped

Heat 3 tablespoons of the oil in a saucepan over a low heat, add the onion and sage and cook until tender but not browned. Leave to cool.

Mash the cheese with the milk to make a smooth spread. Mix in the walnuts and the cooled onions. Chill.

Spread the mixture over the toasted muffins and place under a hot grill for 3–4 minutes or until golden.

Chilli bean

1 tablespoon vegetable oil
1/2 onion, chopped
1/4 teaspoon dried chilli flakes
1 teaspoon ground cumin
1 tablespoon chopped fresh
   coriander
400 g (14 oz) canned black
   beans, chopped
1/2 avocado, sliced
2 tablespoons sour cream
2 tablespoons grated
   Cheddar cheese

Heat the oil in a small frying pan over a low heat, add the onion, chilli, cumin and coriander and cook until the onion is tender. Add the chopped black beans and continue cooking over low heat until the mixture is quite thick.

Spread the beans on the toasted muffins and top with the avocado, sour cream and grated cheese.

Lentil haggis

I was challenged to create a vegetarian dish for Burns night; I decided it had to be a vegetarian haggis, and after many trials and tribulations this is the result. Wild mushrooms add a meaty flavour; they are expensive to buy, but if you pick your own they are a delicious addition.

25 g (1 oz) butter
1 onion, finely chopped
1 garlic clove, crushed
100 g (4 oz) button mushrooms (or wild mushrooms), chopped
400 g (14 oz) brown lentils, cooked
175 g (6 oz) oatmeal
175 g (6 oz) vegetarian suet
2 parsnips, coarsely grated
salt and freshly ground pepper
cayenne pepper
freshly grated nutmeg

Heat the butter in a frying pan, add the onion and garlic and cook until tender Add the mushrooms and cook for 3–4 minutes. Add the cooked lentils and cook for a further 2–3 minutes. Transfer to a bowl and leave to cool.

Spread the oatmeal on a baking sheet and place under a grill to toast to a golden colour, 5–8 minutes. Add the oatmeal to the lentil mixture, together with the vegetarian suet and the grated parsnips. Season well with salt, pepper, cayenne and nutmeg and mix thoroughly.

Lay out a 25 cm (10 inch) square of buttered strong foil and place the lentil mixture in the centre. Roll up the foil and form a ball shape, twisting the ends to seal well.

Tie the foil ball in a damp tea towel or a piece of muslin and steam or poach in simmering water for 45 minutes.

To serve, leave to cool for 5 minutes, then carefully remove the cloth and foil and slice the haggis into neat rounds. Serve on a bed of potato purée and swede purée, in the traditional manner.

Cauliflower and potato curry with mint chutney

4 tablespoons vegetable oil
½ teaspoon turmeric
2 teaspoons ground cumin
1 tablespoon tomato purée
1 cauliflower, cut into florets
½ teaspoon dried chilli flakes
200 g (7 oz) canned tomatoes, drained and chopped
4 potatoes, cut into 2 cm (¾ inch) dice
150ml (¼ pint) vegetable stock
1 teaspoon garam masala

For the mint chutney:
50 g (2 oz) fresh mint, chopped
2 small green chillies, deseeded and chopped
¼ onion, chopped
3 tablespoons fresh lemon juice

Heat the oil in a frying pan, add the turmeric, cumin and tomato purée, reduce the heat and cook for 1–2 minutes. Add the cauliflower and stir to coat with the spices. Add the chilli flakes, tomatoes and potatoes, stir well and leave to cook for a further 4–5 minutes. Pour in the stock, bring to the boil, cover with a lid and simmer gently until the vegetables are tender. Add the garam masala towards the end of the cooking.

Serve with the chutney, made by placing all the ingredients in a liquidizer and blending to a coarse purée.

Aubergine and basil pastitso

Use your favourite standby tomato-based pasta sauce –
you will need about 450–600 g (1–1¼ lb).

1 large aubergine
salt and freshly ground pepper
225 g (8 oz) macaroni
1 large jar of pasta sauce
6 tablespoons olive oil

For the sauce:
40 g (1½ oz) butter
40 g (1½ oz) plain flour
400 ml (14 fl oz) milk
4 tablespoons pesto sauce

Slice the aubergine into 5 mm (¼ inch) slices, spread
on a tray, sprinkle with salt and leave to stand for
30 minutes.

Meanwhile, cook the macaroni in a large
saucepan of boiling salted water until just tender but
still firm to the bite, then drain. Heat the pasta sauce
in a pan, add the macaroni, season to taste and cook
for a further 2 minutes, then set aside.

To make the sauce, melt the butter in a saucepan,
stir in the flour and cook over a low heat for 1–2
minutes. Gradually add the milk and simmer, stirring
all the time, for 2–3 minutes. Set aside.

Preheat the oven to 200°C/400°F/Gas Mark 6.
Rinse the aubergine slices well and pat dry. Brush
with the olive oil and place in the oven until golden
and tender, about 10 minutes, then reduce the oven
heat to 160°C/325°F/Gas Mark 3.

Arrange half the aubergine slices in an ovenproof
dish. Cover with half the macaroni mixture, then
top with the remaining aubergines and finish with
a layer of macaroni. Pour over the white sauce, then
spoon the pesto sauce in lines over the white sauce.
Bake for 30–35 minutes or until golden; serve hot.

Sambusak
(Cheese and potato pasties)

This traditional dish from Syria and the Lebanon is usually made from a type of pizza dough; I use puff pastry for convenience.

4 potatoes
salt and freshly ground pepper
freshly grated nutmeg
2–3 tablespoons cream cheese
1 tablespoon chopped fresh mint
275 g (10 oz) puff pastry
flour for rolling
vegetable oil for frying

Boil the potatoes until just tender. Drain well and leave to go cold. When cold, cut them into 1 cm (½ inch) dice, add the salt and pepper and a little nutmeg and gently stir in the cheese and the mint, taking care not to break up the potatoes.

Roll out the pastry thinly on a lightly floured surface and cut into rounds about 10 cm (4 inches) in diameter, using a pastry cutter or a small saucer as a guide. Put a tablespoon of the filling in the centre of each pastry round and fold the dough over the filling to make a half moon shape.

Crimp the edges together to form small pasties and leave in the refrigerator until required. To serve, fry the pasties in hot oil until golden on both sides. Drain on paper towels and serve hot.

Lentil moussaka tart

175 g (6 oz) lentils, soaked overnight
8 tablespoons vegetable oil
1 onion, finely chopped
1 garlic clove, crushed
1 teaspoon dried thyme
1 teaspoon ground allspice
2 tablespoons tomato purée
2 tablespoons flour
salt and freshly ground pepper
1 large aubergine
1 potato, thinly sliced
1 x 22 cm (9 inch) cooked shortcrust pastry shell

For the cheese sauce:
25 g (1 oz) butter
25 g (1 oz) plain flour
250 ml (8 fl oz) milk
1 teaspoon mustard
50 g (2 oz) cheese, grated

Cook the lentils in about 600 ml (1 pint) water for
30–40 minutes or until tender. Drain and reserve the
cooking liquid; you should have about 300 ml
(½ pint).

Heat 2 tablespoons of the oil in a saucepan, add
the onion and garlic and cook gently until tender.
Increase the heat, add the cooked lentils, the thyme,
allspice and tomato purée and mix well. Cook for a
further 2 minutes. Add the flour and mix in well.
Pour in the reserved lentil cooking liquid a little at a
time to form a sauce around the lentils. Simmer for
10–15 minutes or until the sauce becomes quite
thick. Season to taste and leave to cool.

Preheat the oven to 200°C/400°F/Gas Mark 6.
Make the cheese sauce, following the method on page
114, and beating in the mustard and cheese at the end.

Slice the aubergine lengthways into 1 cm (½ inch)
thick slices. Fry in the remaining oil until golden and

tender. Drain on paper towels and season lightly.
Parboil the potato slices for 2–3 minutes, drain and
pat dry. Fill each aubergine slice with the lentil
mixture, roll them up and place them in the pastry
shell. Arrange the potato slices in overlapping rows
over the aubergine to cover the tart. Pour the sauce
over the potatoes, then place the tart in the oven for
15–20 minutes or until bubbling and golden.

Leeks Portuguese

**A light, colourful, fresh-tasting first course or main
dish. To make a more substantial meal, serve on a
bed of pasta or rice.**

6 tablespoons olive oil
1 onion, finely sliced
1 garlic clove, crushed
450 g (1 lb) young leeks, about 10 cm (4 inches) long
3 tablespoons dry white wine
150 ml (¼ pint) vegetable stock
6 coriander seeds, crushed
200 g (7 oz) canned tomatoes, roughly chopped
sugar
salt and coarsely ground black pepper

Heat the olive oil in a wide saucepan, add the onion
and garlic and cook over a low heat until tender.
Add the leeks and cook for 2 minutes, then pour
in the white wine. Bring to the boil and boil for
1 minute, then add the stock. Cover with a lid and
simmer gently for 5–10 minutes or until the leeks
are tender but not broken up. Using a slotted spoon,
remove the leeks and set aside.
    Add the coriander seeds and tomatoes to the
cooking liquid and boil for 5–10 minutes or until
slightly thickened. Season to taste with a pinch of
sugar, salt and pepper. Return the leeks to the liquid
and leave to cool. Serve at room temperature, sprinkled
with coarsely ground black pepper.

Winter vegetable goulash

4 tablespoons olive oil
1 small cauliflower, cut into florets
3 carrots, cut into 5 mm (1/4 inch) slices
2 tablespoons butter
1 tablespoon caraway seeds
1 garlic clove, crushed
2 turnips, cut into 5 mm (1/4 inch) slices
1 swede, cut into 5 mm (1/4 inch) slices
1 teaspoon paprika
1 tablespoon tomato purée
1 tablespoon plain flour
150 ml (1/4 pint) dry white wine
600 ml (1 pint) vegetable stock
2 courgettes, cut into 5 mm (1/4 inch) slices
1 leek, cut into 5 mm (1/4 inch) slices
salt and freshly ground pepper

Heat 3 tablespoons of the oil in a heavy-bottomed saucepan, add the cauliflower and carrots and cook gently for 2 minutes, without letting them brown.

Add the butter, caraway seeds and garlic and cook for 1 minute, then add the turnips and swede. Sprinkle over the paprika to coat the vegetables. Stir in the tomato purée and flour and cook over a low heat for 2–3 minutes.

Pour in the wine, bring to the boil, and add the vegetable stock. Simmer until the vegetables are just cooked, but still slightly crisp.

Add the courgettes and leek and cook for 2 minutes. Finally add the remaining olive oil. Serve at once, with noodles or rice.

Lentil koftas

150 g (5 oz) lentils, soaked overnight
4 tablespoons vegetable oil
1 green chilli, deseeded and chopped
1 garlic clove, crushed
3 spring onions, shredded
1 tablespoon ground cumin
1/2 tablespoon ground coriander
salt and freshly ground pepper
4 tablespoons rye flour (or plain flour)

For the raita:
1 stick of celery, cut into small dice
75 g (3 oz) cucumber, peeled and cut into small dice
2 tomatoes, halved and cut into small dice
100 ml (3 fl oz) natural yoghurt
2 tablespoons chopped fresh mint

Start making this dish the day before you want to serve it. Place the lentils in a saucepan, cover with cold water and bring to the boil. Skim off any impurities from the surface of the water, then reduce the heat and simmer for 30–40 minutes or until tender. Drain well.

Heat half the oil in a frying pan, add the lentils, chilli and garlic and fry until dry. Add the spring onions, cumin, coriander, salt and pepper and cook for a further 2 minutes.

Add the flour, mix well and cook over a low heat for 3–4 minutes. Leave to cool, then place in the refrigerator overnight.

To make the raita, mix all the ingredients together and chill. Alternatively, make the fruit raita on page 58.

To cook the koftas, heat the remaining oil in a frying pan. Shape the lentil mixture into small ovals and fry gently until golden, about 2 minutes on each side. Serve hot, with the chilled raita.

Savoy cabbage and parsnip jalousie

1 Savoy cabbage
50 g (2 oz) butter
1 onion, thinly sliced
1 teaspoon sugar
1 teaspoon mustard
salt and freshly ground pepper
450 g (1 lb) parsnips, coarsely grated
2 tablespoons caraway seeds
100 g (4 oz) cooked brown rice
50 g (2 oz) Cheddar cheese, grated
2 eggs, beaten
325 g (12 oz) puff pastry
flour for rolling

Remove the outer leaves from the cabbage, blanch them in boiling salted water for 3–4 minutes, refresh under cold water and then dry them well. Roughly shred the remainder of the cabbage.

Heat half the butter in a small frying pan, add the onion and sugar and cook until golden and caramelized. Remove from the heat and leave to cool, then add the mustard and season to taste.

Heat the remaining butter in a frying pan, add the shredded cabbage, grated parsnips and 1 tablespoon caraway seeds; fry for 3–4 minutes or until softened. Transfer to a bowl and leave to cool. Add the rice and cheese and bind the mixture together with one of the eggs.

Preheat the oven to 190°C/375°F/Gas Mark 5.

On a lightly floured surface, roll out the pastry to measure about 20 x 30 cm (8 x 12 inches). Arrange the outer cabbage leaves on the pastry, leaving a 2.5 cm (1 inch) border around the edge. Top with the shredded cabbage mixture. Spoon the caramelized onions along the centre of the filling.

Fold the pastry over and press the edges to seal well. Very carefully lift the pastry roll on to a baking sheet, turning the seam underneath. Brush the pastry all over with the remaining beaten egg and decorate with any pastry trimmings. Brush again with egg, then sprinkle with the remaining caraway seeds. Bake for 20–25 minutes or until cooked and golden brown. Leave to cool for about 5–10 minutes before slicing.

PUDDINGS

Sweet raisin fougasse

15 g (½ oz) fresh yeast
450 g (1 lb) plain flour, sifted
50 g (2 oz) sugar
2 tablespoons olive oil
225 g (8 oz) raisins, soaked in water
1 tablespoon clear honey

Dissolve the yeast in 300 ml (½ pint) warm water and leave for 5 minutes. Mix the flour with the sugar in a large bowl.

Add the oil to the yeast mixture, then add to the flour and mix to form a smooth dough. Leave to rise in a warm, draught-free place for up to 1 hour or until doubled in size.

Pat the raisins dry on paper towels and work into the dough, then leave for a further 30 minutes.

Preheat the oven to 200°C/400°F/Gas Mark 6. Lightly grease a baking sheet. Form the dough into a flat oval shape, place on the baking sheet and bake for about 30 minutes, until risen and golden. Brush with the honey as soon as it comes out of the oven. Leave to cool before serving with lashings of fresh cream. Alternatively this can be made in a loaf tin – and it makes great toast!

Baked plums in red wine syrup

12 ripe Victoria plums, halved and stoned
75 g (3 oz) sugar
150 ml (¼ pint) red wine
juice and grated zest of 1 orange
½ bay leaf
2 cloves

Preheat the oven to 150°C/300°F/Gas Mark 2.

Place the plums in an ovenproof dish and sprinkle with the sugar. Place the wine in a saucepan with the orange juice and zest, bay leaf, cloves and 2 tablespoons water, bring to the boil, boil for 2 minutes, then pour over the plums. Bake for 15–20 minutes or until the plums are tender and the cooking liquid has formed a syrup. (It may be necessary to remove the plums and transfer the liquid to a saucepan to boil until reduced to a coating consistency.)

Serve the plums warm or cold – they are excellent with vanilla ice cream.

Cinnamon baked apples 'en papillote'

These apples formed part of the original £1 menu for four that sparked off the idea for this book.

75 g (3 oz) butter
75 g (3 oz) sugar
½ teaspoon ground cinnamon
2 drops of vanilla essence
juice of ½ orange
4 ripe yellow Golden Delicious apples

Preheat the oven to 190°C/375° F/Gas Mark 5.

Melt the butter in a saucepan, add the sugar, cinnamon, vanilla essence, orange juice and 4 tablespoons water and boil until caramelized to a light sticky syrup.

Core the apples with an apple corer or a melon baller and make a few incisions in the skins to prevent the apples from bursting while they are cooking.

Butter a sheet of foil about 38 cm (15 inches) square and place on a baking sheet (the edges will be overhanging at this stage). Lay the apples on the foil, leaving a gap of about 4 cm (1½ inches) between them. Brush the syrup over the apples, bring the foil up to the top and seal together. Place in the oven and bake for 20–25 minutes or until the apples are tender.

Bring the foil parcel to the table and then undo the foil to release the aroma. Serve the apples with the cooking juices poured over them.

Stuffed apple and rhubarb crumble

600 g (1¼ lb) rhubarb, trimmed and chopped
juice and grated zest of ½ an orange
175 g (6 oz) brown sugar
pinch of ground cinnamon
4 russet (or Golden Delicious) apples
150 g (5 oz) plain flour
1 teaspoon baking powder
75 g (3 oz) blanched almonds, chopped (optional)
75 g (3 oz) butter, diced

Preheat the oven to 180°C/350°F/Gas Mark 4.

Put the rhubarb, orange juice and zest, half the sugar and the cinnamon in a saucepan and bring to the boil. Cover and simmer for 15 minutes. Leave to cool slightly.

Slice off the top 2 cm (¾ inch) of the apples and, using a small teaspoon, carefully scoop out the core and pips from the apples. Fill the apples with the rhubarb mixture.

For the topping, sift the flour and baking powder together. Add the remaining brown sugar and the almonds, if using. Using your fingertips, rub the butter into the flour until the mixture resembles coarse breadcrumbs.

Place the stuffed apples in a buttered ovenproof dish and sprinkle the crumble mixture over the apples. Bake for 35–40 minutes or until the crumble is golden and crisp.

Apple bread and butter pudding

4 tablespoons melted butter
4 slices of white bread (or 4 white crusty rolls)
2 yellow Golden Delicious apples, cored and thinly sliced
100 g (4 oz) raisins
600 ml (1 pint) milk
½ teaspoon vanilla essence
4 eggs
4 tablespoons caster sugar
2 tablespoons apricot jam, warmed
icing sugar to dust

Preheat the oven to 160°C/325°F/Gas Mark 3.
Butter an ovenproof pudding dish.

Butter the bread, then cut each slice into four
triangles; if using rolls, cut them into 5 mm (¼ inch)
thick slices. Arrange the bread in the pudding dish,
overlapping neatly, with the thinly sliced apple
between the slices of bread. Sprinkle over the raisins
and set aside.

Bring the milk to the boil with the vanilla essence.

In a bowl, beat the eggs with the sugar, then carefully pour on the hot milk, a little at a time, whisking
continuously until the mixture forms a smooth custard.
Strain the custard, then pour it over the bread.

Place the pudding dish in a roasting tin containing
about 2.5 cm (1 inch) boiling water and bake for
40 minutes or until just firm to the touch. Remove
from the oven and leave to cool slightly. Brush with
the apricot jam. Just before serving, dust with a little
icing sugar.

Double orange pudding

150 ml (¼ pint) milk
100 g (4 oz) caster sugar
½ teaspoon vanilla essence
juice and grated zest of 1 orange
40 g (1½ oz) butter
40 g (1½ oz) flour
3 eggs, separated
6 tablespoons coarse orange marmalade

Preheat the oven to 180°C/350°F/Gas Mark 4.
Lightly butter four individual ramekin or pudding
moulds (or teacups), about 150 ml (¼ pint) each.

Bring the milk to the boil with half the sugar, the
vanilla essence and the orange zest, then leave to
cool slightly.

In another saucepan, melt the butter and stir in
the flour to form a smooth paste. Cook over a low
heat for about 1 minute, stirring constantly, then
gradually pour in the warm milk, beating well until
smooth. Add the orange juice and cook the sauce
over a low heat for 5–8 minutes, then leave to cool
slightly before beating in the egg yolks.

Whisk the whites until stiff, then fold in the
remaining sugar. Beat half the whites into the sauce,
then carefully fold the sauce into the remaining
whites until evenly combined. Divide the mixture
between the buttered moulds, but do not overfill
them: they should be about two-thirds full.

Place the moulds in a roasting tin containing
about 2 cm (¾ inch) hot water and cook for
20 minutes or until risen and set.

Meanwhile, heat the marmalade in a small
saucepan with 6 tablespoons water to form a sauce.

Turn the puddings out on to warmed serving
plates and serve at once, with the sauce poured over
them. For an elegant presentation, decorate with
orange segments and sprigs of mint.

Orange rice and meringue pudding

15 g (½ oz) butter
50 g (2 oz) Carolina or arborio rice
50 g (2 oz) caster sugar
600 ml (1 pint) milk
grated zest and juice of 1 orange
½ teaspoon vanilla essence
nutmeg

For the meringue:
2 eggs, separated
25 g (1 oz) caster sugar
icing sugar

Preheat the oven to 150°C/300°F/Gas Mark 2.

Butter an ovenproof dish and add the rice and sugar. Bring the milk to the boil with the orange zest and pour over the rice, add the vanilla essence and grate a little nutmeg over the surface. Place in the oven for 1½–2 hours, until the rice is soft.

Add the orange juice, leave to cool slightly, then stir the egg yolks into the rice.

Whisk the egg whites with the caster sugar until stiff peaks form. Spread the egg whites over the rice, dust well with icing sugar and return to the oven for 10–12 minutes or until golden.

Orange honey zabaglione

2 large eggs, separated
225 g (8 oz) clear honey
grated zest and juice of ½ orange
4 tablespoons orange liqueur (optional luxury)

Mix the egg yolks with the honey in a large bowl, add the orange juice and zest (and liqueur if using) and place over a saucepan of simmering water. Whisk constantly until the mixture thickens like a custard and increases 3–4 times in volume.

Remove the mixture from the heat and whisk occasionally until cool. Meanwhile, whisk the egg whites until soft peaks form. Fold them into the honey mixture until thoroughly blended.

Pour into four serving glasses or bowls and chill for up to 4 hours before serving.

Prune and almond frittata

100 g (4 oz) dried prunes, stones removed, soaked overnight
   in cold tea
50 g (2 oz) butter
4 tablespoons brandy (optional luxury)
6 eggs, beaten
4 tablespoons caster sugar
4 tablespoons ground almonds
2 tablespoons flaked almonds
icing sugar to glaze

Preheat the grill.

Cut the prunes into quarters and pat them dry.
Heat the butter in an omelette pan about 15 cm
(6 inches) in diameter. Add the prunes and heat
through for 1 minute. Add the brandy, if using, and
ignite. Shake the pan until the flames die down.

In a bowl, beat the eggs with the sugar and
ground almonds. Pour the egg mixture on to the
prunes and stir gently with a fork over a fairly high
heat until lightly set. Sprinkle over the flaked
almonds and dust with plenty of icing sugar. Place
the pan under the hot grill until the icing sugar
forms a golden glaze.

Turn out on to a warmed serving plate, dust with
a little more icing sugar and serve at once, with a big
spoonful of crème fraîche.

Cinnamon and lemon fritters

6 tablespoons milk
juice and grated zest of 1 lemon
3 tablespoons butter
1/4 teaspoon salt
250 g (9 oz) caster sugar
90 g (3 1/2 oz) plain flour, sifted
2 eggs
vegetable oil for deep-frying
1 teaspoon ground cinnamon

Place the milk, lemon zest, butter, salt and half the sugar in a saucepan and bring to the boil. Add the flour all at once and beat to a smooth paste, using a wooden spoon. Reduce the heat and continue beating until the dough leaves the sides of the pan clean. Leave to cool slightly, then add the eggs one at a time, beating well after each addition.

Heat the oil for deep-frying to 180°C/350°F (until a cube of bread browns in 30 seconds).

Carefully drop teaspoonfuls of the mixture into the hot oil and cook for 4–5 minutes until golden. It is best not to cook too many spoonfuls in each batch. Drain the fritters on paper towels. Mix the remaining sugar with the cinnamon and roll the hot fritters in the cinnamon sugar. Serve hot with vanilla ice cream.

Cinnamon, raisin and oatmeal pancakes

These are my version of a traditional Austrian pudding called Kaiserschmarren. The souffléed pancake mixture is served torn into shreds.

50 g (2 oz) plain flour
1 tablespoon baking powder
½ teaspoon ground cinnamon
40 g (1½ oz) porridge oats
1 tablespoon sugar
150 ml (¼ pint) milk
4 tablespoons melted butter
2 eggs, separated
50 g (2 oz) raisins, soaked overnight in a little water
icing sugar to dust
150 g (5 oz) fruit compote (apple, plum or apricot)

Preheat the oven to 190°C/375°F/Gas Mark 5.

Mix the flour, baking powder, cinnamon, oats and sugar in a bowl. Mix in the milk, half the melted butter and the egg yolks.

Beat the egg whites until stiff and fold into the batter, together with the raisins. Heat the remaining butter in a flameproof dish, approximately 25 cm (10 inches) diameter. Pour in the batter and place in the oven for 8–10 minutes, until just firm. Tear into pieces with two forks and divide between four serving plates. Dust well with icing sugar and serve with fruit compote.

Macaroon pancakes with hot cherries

175 g (6 oz) plain flour
pinch of salt
pinch of sugar
1 egg
2 egg yolks
5 tablespoons vegetable oil
375 ml (12 fl oz) milk
45 g (1½ oz) almond macaroon biscuits, crushed
400 g (14 oz) canned cherries in syrup
4 tablespoons vodka or, better still, cherry vodka
    (optional luxury)
icing sugar to dust

Sift the flour and salt into a large bowl and add the sugar, egg and yolks, 3 tablespoons of the vegetable oil and half the milk. Whisk until smooth, then add the remaining milk.

Strain into a clean bowl or large jug, then stir in the crushed macaroons.

Heat a little of the remaining oil in a frying pan until it is very hot, then pour away. Add a thin layer of the batter and tilt the pan to coat the base evenly and thinly.

Cook over medium-high heat until lightly coloured underneath. Toss the pancake or turn it over with a palette knife and cook the other side. Turn out on to a plate and keep warm while you make pancakes with the rest of the batter.

Heat the cherries in their syrup, adding the vodka if you like, and use to fill the pancakes. Fold them up carefully and serve dusted with icing sugar. A big spoonful of sour cream will not go amiss.

Rhubarb and polenta tart

100 g (4 oz) sugar
400 g (14 oz) rhubarb, peeled and cut into 5 cm (2 inch)
  lengths
4 tablespoons plain flour
4 tablespoons polenta
4 tablespoons soft brown sugar
½ teaspoon ground cinnamon
50 g (2 oz) cold butter, cut into small pieces
1 x 22 cm (9 inch) sweetcrust pastry shell

Preheat the oven to 180°C/350°F/Gas Mark 4.

Place the sugar in a saucepan with 150 ml (¼ pint) water, bring to the boil and boil for 2 minutes. Add the rhubarb and simmer for 2 minutes longer. Drain and set aside.

Place the flour, polenta, brown sugar, cinnamon and butter in a liquidizer or food processor and pulse until the mixture resembles coarse breadcrumbs.

Place the drained rhubarb in the pastry shell and sprinkle over the polenta crumble mixture. Place in the oven for about 20 minutes or until the topping is golden and crisp.

Treacle tart

300 ml (½ pint) golden syrup
75 g (3 oz) porridge oats
grated zest and juice of 1 lemon
pinch of ground ginger
1 x 22 cm (9 inch) sweetcrust pastry shell

Preheat the oven to 200°C/400°F/Gas Mark 6.

In a saucepan, gently warm the golden syrup.
Stir in the oats and add the lemon juice and zest and
the ginger. Heat the mixture until it is slightly runny.

Pour into the pastry shell and bake for about 25
minutes. Leave to cool for 5–10 minutes (the filling
will firm up as it cools). Serve warm or cold with
fresh cream.

Bread and jam soufflé

50 g (2 oz) butter
6 slices of white bread, crusts removed and cut into triangles
50 ml (2 fl oz) rum (optional)
150 g (5 oz) fruit jam (cherry, strawberry or raspberry)
4 eggs, separated
50 g (2 oz) icing sugar
40 g (1½ oz) flour

Melt the butter in a frying pan, add the bread and fry until golden. Place in an ovenproof dish about 20 x 12 cm (8 x 5 inches) and 2.5 cm (1 inch) deep. Pour over the rum, if using, to lightly soak the bread. Spoon over the jam and set aside.

In a bowl, beat the egg whites with the sugar until stiff. Remove about a quarter of the egg whites into another bowl. Add the yolks to this and beat until smooth. Sift the flour over the first bowl of egg whites. Fold the yolk mixture into the whites and, using a spatula, fold together lightly to blend evenly while keeping air in the mixture.

Scoop the mixture over the fried bread and jam, then dust the top with more icing sugar and bake for 8–10 minutes or until golden. Take care as it may colour very quickly. Serve immediately.

Clafoutis of plums and raisins

2 eggs
1 egg yolk
50 g (2 oz) caster sugar
40 g (1½ oz) plain flour
275 ml (9 fl oz) milk
2 drops of vanilla essence
40 g (1½ oz) butter, melted
450 g (1 lb) fresh ripe plums, halved, stoned and
   cut into pieces
3-4 tablespoons brown sugar
icing sugar to dust

Preheat the oven to 180°C/350°F/Gas Mark 4.

Place the eggs, egg yolk and caster sugar in a
bowl and beat together until light. Gradually sift in
the flour and beat to obtain a smooth batter. Add
the milk, the vanilla essence and 25 g (1 oz) of the
melted butter and beat again until smooth.

Heat the remaining butter in a flameproof oven
dish, about 20 x 12 cm (8 x 5 inches). Add the plums
and brown sugar and cook for 1 minute, then pour
on the batter.

Place in the oven and cook until golden and set,
yet still light and soft inside. Dust with icing sugar
and serve with cream or clotted cream.

Baked fruit kebabs
with chocolate couscous

2 oranges
2 bananas
1 ripe pear
4 pitted prunes, soaked and halved
4 tablespoons sugar
2 tablespoons rum

For the couscous:
200 ml (7 fl oz) milk
40 g (1½ oz) sugar
½ tablespoon cocoa powder
100 g (4 oz) couscous
2 tablespoons rum (optional luxury)

For the couscous, heat the milk and sugar in a small saucepan, add the cocoa, stir well and bring to the boil. Place the couscous in a bowl, pour over the chocolate milk, stir well, then cover and leave to stand for 5–8 minutes. Separate the grains of couscous with a fork, cover and leave for a further 5 minutes. Stir once again, add the rum, if using, and leave in the refrigerator.

Soak four bamboo skewers in cold water for about 30 minutes. Preheat the oven to 230°C/450°F/Gas Mark 8.

Peel the oranges, bananas and pear. Cut each banana into eight thick slices. Cut the oranges into quarters and cut the pear in half, remove the core, then cut into quarters.

Thread the fruit on to the skewers, with the prune halves at each end of the skewers. Place the fruit skewers in a shallow ovenproof dish.

Boil the sugar with 2 tablespoons water for 5 minutes, then pour over the fruit skewers. Add the rum, if using, and bake in the hot oven for 5 minutes, basting from time to time.

Serve the chilled couscous on a platter, topped with the hot fruit kebabs. Spoon over a little of the hot syrup from the baking dish. Vanilla ice cream or fruit sorbet are a good accompaniment.

Coffee risotto

2 tablespoons Camp coffee or 1 tablespoon instant coffee powder
grated zest and juice of ½ orange
100 g (4 oz) arborio rice
600 ml (1 pint) milk
2 drops of vanilla essence
100 g (4 oz) caster sugar
25 g (1 oz) butter
175 ml (6 fl oz) whipping cream
2 tablespoons rum (optional)

Place the coffee and orange juice in a saucepan with 150 ml (¼ pint) water and bring to the boil. Remove from the heat, add the rice and leave to soak for 5 minutes.

Return the pan to the heat and add the milk and vanilla essence. Cook over a low heat until the rice is tender, but still slightly firm to the bite.

Remove from the heat, add the sugar, orange zest, butter, cream and rum (if using), stir through gently and serve at once.

Coffee custards

600 ml (1 pint) milk
½ teaspoon vanilla essence
4 tablespoons coffee essence
2 large eggs
100 g (4 oz) caster sugar

Preheat the oven to 160°C/325°F/Gas Mark 3.

Bring the milk to the boil with the vanilla and coffee essence.

Whisk the eggs and the sugar together in a bowl. Pour on the boiled milk a little at a time, whisking constantly. Strain through a fine strainer, then pour into four individual ramekin moulds.

Place in a shallow dish, then pour boiling water around and halfway up the side of the ramekins.

Place in the oven and cook for about 45 minutes or until just set. Leave to cool completely. Turn out of the moulds. Decorate with whipped cream if you feel naughty.

Poached pears in espresso-cardamom syrup

4 firm but ripe dessert pears (preferably Williams)
300 ml (½ pint) strong coffee (espresso)
150 g (5 oz) sugar
6 cardamom pods, crushed
juice and grated zest of ½ lemon
2 tablespoons flaked almonds, toasted
sprigs of mint to decorate

Peel the pears neatly, using a potato peeler, leaving the stalks intact and keeping the shape of the pear. Cut a little off the base of each pear to help it remain upright while it is poaching.

Choose a saucepan that will hold the four pears upright side by side. Put the coffee, sugar, 75 ml (3 fl oz) water, cardamom and lemon juice and zest in the pan and bring to the boil, stirring until the sugar has dissolved. Add the pears, cover the pan, reduce the heat and simmer for about 20–25 minutes or until the pears are tender but still retaining their shape.

Using a slotted spoon, remove the pears from the syrup and transfer to a bowl. Boil the syrup rapidly until reduced to about 125 ml (4 fl oz). Leave to cool, then pour the syrup over the pears and place in the refrigerator for up to 4 hours, to chill thoroughly.

Serve the pears with the coffee syrup, sprinkle over the toasted almonds and decorate with the mint. Serve with crème fraîche or vanilla yoghurt.

Vol-au-vents of pineapple with curry ice cream

250 g (9 oz) puff pastry
1 egg yolk, beaten
25 g (1 oz) butter
1 teaspoon finely shredded fresh root ginger
400 g (14 oz) canned pineapple rings, cut into dice,
    syrup reserved

For the curry ice cream:
300 ml (½ pint) creamy milk
1 tablespoon curry powder
4 egg yolks
100 g (4 oz) caster sugar

For the ice cream, bring the milk to the boil with
the curry powder for 30 seconds, then leave to cool
slightly. In a large bowl, whisk the egg yolks with
the sugar until pale and doubled in volume. Pour the
spiced milk slowly on to the eggs, beating all the
time. Stir occasionally until cool.

When cold, pour into an ice cream machine
and freeze. Alternatively, if you do not have an ice
cream maker, pour the ice cream into a shallow
container and place in the freezer, stirring occasionally until frozen.

Preheat the oven to 200°C/400°F/Gas Mark 6.

For the vol-au-vents, roll out the pastry about
5 mm (¼ inch) thick. Cut out four circles with an
8 cm (3 inch) diameter cutter. Using a cutter just a
little smaller than the 8 cm (3 inch) one, mark the
top of each circle, then use a sharp knife to mark a
criss-cross pattern in the inner circle.

Place the four pastry circles on a baking sheet,
brush with a little beaten egg yolk and leave to rest
for up to 30 minutes. Bake the pastry in the oven

until golden. Leave in a cool place until cold,
then carefully remove the lids and scoop out any
uncooked pastry from within.

Heat half the butter in a frying pan, add the ginger
and cook for 1 minute without letting it brown. Add
the diced pineapple and sauté until golden. Add the
reserved syrup and boil to reduce with the pineapple.
Swirl in the remaining butter to form a light sauce
around the pineapple. Spoon the pineapple into the
vol-au-vents and serve with the ice cream.

Asian toffee rice pudding

50 g (2 oz) butter
75 g (3 oz) demerara sugar
$\frac{1}{4}$ teaspoon ground cinnamon
10 cardamom pods, shelled and seeds crushed
pinch of freshly grated nutmeg
75 g (3 oz) ground rice
1 litre (1$\frac{3}{4}$ pints) milk
25 g (1 oz) sultanas

Heat the butter and sugar together in a saucepan
until slightly caramelized. Add the spices and the rice
and stir well.

Add the milk a little at a time, stirring well to
prevent lumps from forming. When all the milk has
been added, reduce the heat, add the sultanas and
cook over a low heat for about 25 minutes. If the
pudding becomes too thick, add a little more milk.
Serve hot or cold. I particularly like this dessert
served cold with a compote of apricots, topped with
toasted almonds.

Sweetcorn ice cream with summer berry compote

3 egg yolks
1 egg
150 g (5 oz) caster sugar
400 ml (14 fl oz) milk
200 ml (7 fl oz) double cream
175 g (6 oz) canned sweetcorn kernels, puréed

For the compote:
3 tablespoons sugar
400 g (14 oz) mixed berries (strawberries, blackberries, raspberries)
sprigs of mint to decorate

To make the ice cream, whisk the egg yolks, egg and sugar until pale and doubled in volume. Boil the milk and cream together, then leave to cool slightly. Pour the hot milk a little at a time on to the egg mixture, stirring all the time. Add the puréed sweetcorn and strain through a sieve.

Return the mixture to the saucepan and cook over a low heat, stirring constantly, until the mixture thickens enough to coat the back of a spoon (do not let it boil.)

Cool the mixture quickly. When cold, pour into an ice cream machine and freeze. When the ice cream is set, transfer it to a plastic container and place in the freezer.

To make the compote, place the sugar in a saucepan with 3 tablespoons water, bring to the boil, add the berries and remove from the heat. Cover and leave to cool completely.

Before serving let the ice cream soften a little at room temperature. Spoon the fruit compote into individual soup plates. Top with a ball of the sweetcorn ice cream and decorate with sprigs of mint.

Caramelized bananas with coconut fried ice cream

500 ml (16 fl oz) vanilla ice cream
1 egg, beaten
75 g (3 oz) plain flour, sifted
4 tablespoons desiccated coconut
4 tablespoons fresh white breadcrumbs
4 bananas
6 tablespoons maple syrup
6 tablespoons fresh orange juice
2 tablespoons fresh lemon juice
2 tablespoons rum (optional luxury)
vegetable oil for deep-frying

Prepare the ice cream the day before you want to serve this dish. Using an ice cream scoop, scoop four balls of ice cream and place in the freezer on a sheet of foil. Prepare a thick batter by beating together the egg, flour and 4–5 tablespoons water. Mix the desiccated coconut with the breadcrumbs in a shallow dish. Dip the ice cream balls in the batter, then roll them in the coconut mixture to coat them thickly and evenly. Return to the freezer and freeze overnight.

Shortly before serving, peel the bananas and cut each one in half lengthways. Heat the maple syrup, orange and lemon juice, and rum, if using, in a frying pan over a moderate heat. Add the bananas and cook for 3–4 minutes, adding a little water if necessary, so that the bananas are caramelized, warmed through and surrounded by a light syrup.

Heat the oil until a cube of bread browns in 30 seconds. Fry the ice cream balls until they are just golden. Serve at once, with the bananas and the caramelized juices.

Banana 'Wednesday'

Why save a sundae for Sunday?

4 bananas
4 scoops of chocolate ice cream
1 tablespoon flaked almonds, toasted
sprigs of mint to decorate

For the caramel sauce:
40 g (1½ oz) soft brown sugar
3 tablespoons double cream
40 g (1½ oz) unsalted butter
¼ teaspoon vanilla essence

Preheat the oven to 200°C/400°F/Gas Mark 6.

Place the bananas in their skins on a baking sheet
and bake for 5–8 minutes or until they are warmed
through but not soft.

Meanwhile, prepare the sauce. Place the sugar,
cream, butter and vanilla essence in a heavy-bottomed
saucepan and cook, stirring, for 3–5 minutes or until
the mixture turns a light caramel colour.

Peel the bananas and cut them in half lengthways
or into slices.

Place the chocolate ice cream in individual dishes,
top with the roasted bananas and pour over the
caramel sauce. Sprinkle over the toasted almonds
and decorate with the mint.

Lemonade granita with raspberry sauce

6 juicy lemons
150 g (5 oz) sugar
225 g (8 oz) can raspberries (or fresh, in season)
1 tablespoon caster sugar
raspberries and sprigs of mint to decorate

Finely grate the zest of one of the lemons. Squeeze the juice from all the lemons. Place the sugar, 450 ml (¾ pint) water and the lemon zest in a saucepan, bring to the boil, reduce the heat and simmer until the sugar has dissolved. Add the lemon juice and leave to cool.

Pour the liquid into a shallow dish (preferably stainless steel) approximately 15 cm (6 inches) square and place in the freezer.

After 30 minutes or so the liquid will start to set on the surface and around the edge of the dish. Using a fork, scrape it until the loose crystals of ice are evenly distributed. Return to the freezer for a further 30 minutes. Repeat the scraping process twice more.

Place the raspberries in a liquidizer with the caster sugar and blend to a purée. Rub through a sieve to remove any pips.

To serve, scoop the lemon granita into individual glasses, pour over the raspberry sauce and decorate with raspberries and mint.

Blackberry ice cream soda

I'm sure many of you remember enjoying ice cream soda when you were young. Here is a real taste of nostalgia and late-summer simplicity.

325 g (12 oz) fresh blackberries (buy or pick your own)
a little caster sugar
4 scoops of vanilla ice cream
300 ml (½ pint) cream soda

Sweeten the blackberries with a little sugar if required. Divide the berries between four tall glasses and top with the ice cream. Pour over the soda and serve immediately, while it is still bubbling.

almonds: prune and almond frittata, 132
anchovies, braised chicken with olives and, 89
  salmon cakes with anchovy aïoli, 88
apples: apple bread and butter pudding, 128
  cinnamon baked apples 'en papillote', 126
  stuffed apple and rhubarb crumble, 127
arrancini, 49
Asian spiced herrings with fruit raita, 58
Asian toffee rice pudding, 145
aubergines: aubergine and basil pastitso, 114
  lentil moussaka tart, 116
avgolemono, 21

bacon: B.L.T. salad, 45
  caraway, onion and bacon tart, 38
  penne with spring vegetables and mint, 67
baked beans: spicy Mexican barbecue bean soup, 27
bananas: banana 'Wednesday', 148
  caramelized bananas with coconut fried
    ice cream, 147
  fruit raita, 58
bang bang potatoes, 109
barbecue spice rub chicken, 91
batter pudding, spicy herb sausages in, 98
beetroot 'gravad mackerel', 50
bisque, pumpkin, 18
black beans: chilli bean muffin pizzas, 111
  grilled chicken wings on drunken black
    beans with chilli verde, 90
  Mexican dirty rice salad, 40
black pudding, cabbage and turnip soup, 24
blackberry ice cream soda, 150
B.L.T. salad, 45
blue cheese and walnut muffin pizzas, 111
bourride of smoked haddock, 78
bread: bread and butter pudding, apple, 128
  bread and jam soufflé, 138
broad bean and lemongrass vichyssoise, 23
bstila of chicken with sweet spices, 94

cabbage: braised blade of pork, 100
  cabbage, turnip and black pudding soup, 24
  Savoy cabbage and parsnip jalousie, 120
cannellini beans: cod tagine, 85
  rigatoni with white bean hummus, 64
  white bean hummus with yoghurt, 39
caramel sauce, 148
caramelized bananas with coconut fried
    ice cream, 147
caraway, onion and bacon tart, 38
cauliflower and potato curry with mint
    chutney, 113
ceviche of whiting, 48
chargrilled calamari salad, 46
  mackerel with spicy tomato chutney, 87
cheese: blue cheese and walnut muffin pizzas, 111
  parsley mash gnocchi with blue cheese, 65
  sambusak (cheese and potato pasties), 115
cherries: macaroon pancakes with hot cherries, 135
chicken: barbecue spice rub chicken, 91
  braised chicken with anchovies and olives, 89
  bstila of chicken with sweet spices, 94
  chicken and mustard pot pie, 93
  grilled chicken wings on drunken black
    beans with chilli verde, 90
  Palak chicken, 92
  Thai chicken broth, 28
  Thai chicken wings in spiced coconut milk, 37
  see also liver

chickpeas: jumbled pasta, chickpea and basil
    salad, 42
chillies: chilli bean muffin pizzas, 111
  chocolate chilli glazed pork, 99
  grilled chicken wings on drunken black
    beans with chilli verde, 90
chocolate: baked fruit kebabs with chocolate
    couscous, 140
  chocolate chilli glazed pork, 99
chowder, mussel, 19
chutney, mint, 113
  spicy tomato, 87
cinnamon and lemon fritters, 133
  cinnamon baked apples 'en papillote', 126
  cinnamon, raisin and oatmeal pancakes, 134
clafoutis of plums and raisins, 139
coconut fried ice cream, caramelized
    bananas with, 147
coconut milk, Thai chicken wings in, 37
cod: baked cod with tomato and mustard sauce, 82
  cod tagine, 85
  fresh salt cod on herb-braised potatoes, 84
coffee: coffee custards, 142
  coffee risotto, 141
  poached pears in espresso-cardamom
    syrup, 143
corn: *see* sweetcorn
courgettes, crushed sweetcorn risotto with, 75
couscous: baked fruit kebabs with chocolate
    couscous, 140
crostini, herring, 25
cumin and ginger ketchup, 83
curries: cauliflower and potato curry with
    mint chutney, 113
  curry ice cream, 144
  Oriental mushroom fritters with peanut
    curry dip, 35

dal soup with toasted cumin and rocket oil, 30
daube of rabbit with orange, cinnamon and
    rosemary, 97
dips: peanut curry dip, 35
  verdura tonnato, 43
  white bean hummus, 39

eggs: avgolemono (Greek egg and lemon soup), 21
  baked tomatoes with coddled eggs, 36
  kedgeree in filo purses, 79
  open pasta with scrambled eggs and
    mussels, 71
  potato tortilla with rosemary and lemon, 108
  prune and almond frittata, 132

fettuccine with charred tomatoes and
    rosemary oil, 63
filo purses, kedgeree in, 79
fishburgers, Shanghai, 83
fougasse, sweet raisin, 124
French onion soup with herring crostini, 25
frittata, prune and almond, 132
fritters: cinnamon and lemon, 133
  Oriental mushroom, 35
fusilli, hot dog, 70

garlic: garlic mushroom muffin pizzas, 110
  linguine with garlic-chilli oil, 72
  tourin blanchi (garlic soup), 26
gazpacho, green tomato, 22
gnocchi, parsley mash with blue cheese, 65

goulash, winter vegetable, 118
granita, lemonade, 149
Greek egg and lemon soup, 21
green beans: spaghetti with potatoes and
    wilted beans, 68
grey mullet in 'acqua pazza', 81
guacamole, chunky pea, 20

haddock: see smoked haddock
haggis, lentil, 112
herrings: Asian spiced herrings with fruit raita, 58
    French onion soup with herring crostini, 25
    oatmeal fried herrings, 59
    see also roes
horseradish mash, caveached sardines on, 57
hot dog fusilli, 70
hummus: rigatoni with white bean hummus, 64
    white bean hummus with yoghurt, 39

ice cream: banana 'Wednesday', 148
    blackberry ice cream soda, 150
    caramelized bananas with coconut fried
        ice cream, 147
    curry ice cream, 144
    sweetcorn ice cream with summer berry
        compote, 146

jam: bread and jam soufflé, 138

kebabs: baked fruit kebabs with chocolate
        couscous, 140
kedgeree in filo purses, 79
koftas, lentil, 119
    Persian (lamb) koftas with pitta toasts, 103
Korean-style barbecue lamb ribs, 102

lamb: Korean-style barbecue lamb ribs, 102
    lamb short ribs with Tunisian spices, 105
    Mexican lamb pasties, 104
    Persian koftas with pitta toasts, 103
lasagne: open pasta with scrambled eggs
        and mussels, 71
leeks: frozen broad bean and lemongrass
        vichyssoise, 23
    leeks Portuguese, 117
lemon: avgolemono (Greek egg and lemon
        soup), 21
    cinnamon and lemon fritters, 133
    lemonade granita with raspberry sauce, 149
lentils: dal soup with toasted cumin and
        rocket oil, 30
    lentil haggis, 112
    lentil koftas, 119
    lentil moussaka tart, 116
linguine with garlic-chilli oil, 72
liver: B.L.T. salad, 45
    chicken liver risotto, 74
    spaghetti with chicken liver sauce, 69

macaroon pancakes with hot cherries, 135
macaroni: aubergine and basil pastitso, 114
mackerel: beetroot 'gravad mackerel', 50
    chargrilled mackerel with spicy tomato
        chutney, 87
    grilled mackerel with sweet and sour
        rhubarb, 86
Malaysian vegetable salad, 41
mayonnaise: soft roe potato cakes with caper
        mayo, 52
    verdura tonnato, 43

meatballs: Peking style meatballs with
        noodles, 73
    Persian koftas with pitta toasts, 103
meringue: orange rice and meringue pudding, 130
Mexican barbecue bean soup, 27
Mexican dirty rice salad, 40
    lamb pasties, 104
mint chutney, 113
moussaka tart, lentil, 116
muffin pizzas, 110
mullet: see grey mullet
mushrooms: garlic mushroom muffin pizzas, 110
    lentil haggis, 112
    Oriental mushroom fritters with peanut
        curry dip, 35
    pesto baked mushrooms, 34
mussels: grilled stuffed mussels with pico
        de gallo, 54
    mussel chowder, 19
    open pasta with scrambled eggs and
        mussels, 71
    Thai mussels, 55

nettle: callaloo with crispy lardons, 29
noodles: Peking style meatballs with noodles, 73

oatmeal: cinamon, raisin and oatmeal
        pancakes, 134
    fried herrings, 59
    lentil haggis, 112
omelettes: potato tortilla with rosemary
        and lemon, 108
    prune and almond frittata, 132
onions: caraway, onion and bacon tart, 38
    French onion soup with herring crostini, 25
orange honey zabaglione, 131
    orange pudding, double, 129
    orange rice and meringue pudding, 130
Oriental mushroom fritters with peanut
        curry dip, 35
osso buco, turkey, 96

pancakes: cinnamon, raisin and oatmeal
        pancakes, 134
    macaroon pancakes with hot cherries, 135
parsley mash gnocchi with blue cheese, 65
parsnips: Savoy cabbage and parsnip jalousie, 120
pasta, 62-73
pasties: Mexican lamb pasties, 104
    sambusak (cheese and potato pasties), 115
pastitso, aubergine and basil, 114
peanut curry dip, Oriental mushroom fritters
        with, 35
pears: poached pears in espresso-cardamom
        syrup, 143
pea guacamole, 20
Peking style meatballs with noodles, 73
penne: penne with caramelized celery, walnut
        and sage gremolata, 62
    penne with spring vegetables and mint, 67
Persian koftas with pitta toasts, 103
pesto baked mushrooms, 34
pineapple: vol-au-vents of pineapple with
        curry ice cream, 144
pitta toasts, Persian koftas with, 103
pizzas, muffin, 110
plaice: baked plaice with sardine tapenade, 80
plums: baked plums in red wine syrup, 125
    clafoutis of plums and raisins, 139
polenta: rhubarb and polenta tart, 136

pork: braised blade of pork, 100
  chocolate chilli glazed pork, 99
  Peking style meatballs with noodles, 73
potatoes: bang bang potatoes, 109
  cauliflower and potato curry with mint
    chutney, 113
  caveached sardines on horseradish mash, 57
  fresh salt cod on herb-braised potatoes, 84
  parsley mash gnocchi with blue cheese, 65
  potato tortilla with rosemary and lemon, 108
  sambusak (cheese and potato pasties), 115
  soft roe potato cakes with caper mayo, 52
  spaghetti with potatoes and wilted beans, 68
prunes: braised blade of pork, 100
  prune and almond frittata, 132
puddings, 124–150
pumpkin bisque, 18

rabbit: daube of rabbit with orange, cinnamon
    and rosemary, 97
raisins: cinnamon, raisin and oatmeal
    pancakes, 134
  clafoutis of plums and raisins, 139
  sweet raisin fougasse, 124
raita, fruit, 58
  celery, 119
raspberry sauce, lemonade granita with, 149
red cabbage: braised blade of pork, 100
rhubarb: grilled mackerel with sweet and sour
    rhubarb, 86
  rhubarb and polenta tart, 136
  stuffed apple and rhubarb crumble, 127
rice: arrancini, 49
  Asian toffee rice pudding, 145
  kedgeree in filo purses, 79
  Mexican dirty rice salad, 40
  orange rice and meringue pudding, 130
  see also risotto
rigatoni with white bean hummus, 64
risotto: chicken liver, 74
  coffee, 141
  crushed sweetcorn with courgettes, 75
rocket oil, dal soup with toasted cumin and, 30
roes: roes on toast, 53
  soft roe potato cakes with caper mayo, 52

salads: B.L.T., 45
  chargrilled calamari, 46
  crispy Malaysian vegetable, 41
  Italian tuna and white bean, 47
  jumbled pasta, chickpea and basil, 42
  Mexican dirty rice, 40
  sardines 'Monégasque', 44
salmon: arrancini, 49
  cakes with anchovy aïoli, 88
sambusak (cheese and potato pasties), 45
sardines: baked plaice with sardine tapenade, 80
  caveached sardines on horseradish mash, 57
  salad of sardines 'Monégasque', 44
  tatin of sardines, 56
sausages: hot dog fusilli, 70
  spicy herb sausages in batter pudding, 98
Savoy cabbage and parsnip jalousie, 120
Shanghai fishburgers with cumin and ginger
    ketchup, 89
smoked haddock: bourride of, 78
  kedgeree in filo purses, 79
soups, 18–31
soufflé: bread and jam, 138

spaghetti with chicken liver sauce, 69
  with potatoes and wilted beans, 68
spinach: Palak chicken, 92
squid: chargrilled calamari salad, 46
stinging nettles: callaloo with crispy lardons, 29
sweetcorn: crushed sweetcorn risotto with
    courgettes, 75
  roasted corn broth, 20
  sweetcorn ice cream with summer berry
    compote, 146
tagine, cod, 85
tapenade, sardine, 80
tarts: caraway, onion and bacon tart, 38
  lentil moussaka tart, 116
  rhubarb and polenta tart, 136
  tatin of sardines, 56
  treacle tart, 137
Thai chicken broth, 28
Thai chicken wings in spiced coconut milk, 37
Thai mussels, 55
toffee rice pudding, Asian, 145
tomatoes: baked cod with tomato and mustard
    sauce, 82
  baked tomatoes with coddled eggs, 36
  B.L.T. salad, 45
  chargrilled mackerel with spicy tomato
    chutney, 87
  fettuccine with charred tomatoes and
    rosemary oil, 63
  green tomato gazpacho, 22
  grey mullet in 'acqua pazza', 81
  grilled stuffed mussels with pico de gallo, 54
  hot dog fusilli, 70
  leeks Portuguese, 117
  Napoletana muffin pizzas, 110
  trenette with tuna and tomatoes, 66
tortilla, potato with rosemary and lemon, 108
tourin blanchi (garlic soup), 26
treacle tart, 137
trenette with tuna and tomatoes, 66
tuna: Italian tuna and white bean salad, 47
  trenette with tuna and tomatoes, 66
  verdura tonnato, 43
turkey osso buco, 96
turnips: cabbage, turnip and black pudding
    soup, 24

vegetarian dishes, 108–121
verdura tonnato, 43
vichyssoise, frozen broad bean and
    lemongrass, 23
vol-au-vents: of pineapple with curry
    ice cream, 144

walnuts: blue cheese and walnut muffin pizzas, 111
  penne with caramelized celery, walnut
    and sage gremolata, 62
white bean hummus with yoghurt, 39
  Italian tuna and white bean salad, 47
whiting: ceviche of whiting, 48
  Shanghai fishburgers with cumin and
    ginger ketchup, 89
wine: baked plums in red wine syrup, 125
winter vegetable goulash, 118

yoghurt: fruit raita, 58
  white bean hummus with, 39

zabaglione, orange honey, 131

Acknowledgements

A million thanks to my wife, Anita, whose help and patience behind the scenes has been truly invaluable, and to my children Lee, Ryan, Lauren and Rosie, to whom the book is dedicated.

I would very much like to thank the following people for their invaluable contributions to this book: Bridget Sargeson and Jane Suthering, food stylists, and Julian Marshall, my executive sous-chef, who between them prepared the dishes for photography; I thank them all immensely.

Photographer Philip Wilkins, for the care and true professionalism that went into each photograph, which is evident in the final product.

Sue Russell, for her beautiful photographic props and materials.

All at Weidenfeld & Nicolson, particularly Nick Clark and Maggie Ramsay, and Editorial Director Susan Haynes, for her belief and interest in the idea.

Geoffrey Gelardi, Managing Director at The Lanesborough, for his continuing support and encouragement in my new projects.

Finally, I must not forget to thank Simon Hinde, Consumer Affairs Correspondent for the *Sunday Times*, who set the challenge in 1995 that set the whole idea of this book in motion.